Cabin *fever*

20 Modern Log Cabin Quilts

Natalia Bonner and Kathleen Whiting

stashBOOKS®

an imprint of C&T Publishing

Text copyright © 2015 by Natalia Bonner and Kathleen Whiting

Photography and artwork copyright © 2015 by C&T Publishing, Inc.

Publisher: Amy Marson

Creative Director: Gailen Runge

Art Director: Kristy Zacharias

Editors: S. Michele Fry and Karla Menaugh

Technical Editors: Nan Powell and Sadhana Wray

Cover/Book Designer: April Mostek

Production Coordinator: Freesia Pearson Blizard

Production Editor: Joanna Burgarino

Illustrators: Zinnia Heinzmann and Rue Flaherty

Photo Assistant: Mary Peyton Peppo

Styled photography by Nissa Brehmer and instructional photography by Diane Pedersen, unless otherwise noted

Published by Stash Books, an imprint of C&T Publishing, Inc., P.O. Box 1456, Lafayette, CA 94549

Library of Congress Cataloging-in-Publication Data

Bonner, Natalia, 1982-

  Cabin fever : 20 modern log cabin quilts / Natalia Bonner & Kathleen Whiting.

    pages cm

  ISBN 978-1-61745-030-3 (soft cover)

  1. Quilting--Patterns. 2. Patchwork--Patterns. 3. Log cabin quilts. I. Whiting, Kathleen, 1959- II. Title.

  TT835.B6263 2015

  746.46--dc23

                    2014036814

Printed in the USA

10 9 8 7 6 5 4 3 2

Dedication

This is for you, our online and local quilting friends and family! Your kind words and support keep us designing and creating beautiful quilts. You give us the desire to work at what we both love.

Acknowledgments

Brad and John, thanks for letting us do what we love.

Special thanks to Moda Fabrics, Art Gallery Fabrics, FreeSpirit Fabrics, Birch Fabrics, and Michael Miller Fabrics, and to your talented fabric designers. The fabrics you have provided for this book are beautiful and have helped us to create these wonderful quilts.

Thank you, Ilene Peterson and Emmy Jasperson. Your help in piecing the quilts in this book was more appreciated than you'll ever know.

Thank you, C&T Publishing / Stash Books. You have believed in us, and you have made the process great and the ride easy.

Contents

Introduction

Log Cabin quilts are the most recognized quilts in history. Just as architecture has changed from the log cabin to the modern home of today, so has quilting. Yet while we've gone from hand quilting to advanced technology, the basics of construction of a Log Cabin block have stayed the same. You start with a strong foundation, or the center block in the Log Cabin block, and then add "logs," or strips, to the foundation. Today, colors, size, and shape have changed our home construction as well as our quiltmaking.

Early Log Cabin blocks were hand stitched and made on a foundation. The center block was red, which represented the hearth of the home. The logs, or strips, were then placed in a sequence around the center block. Generally the logs were light and dark fabrics, which represented the sunny and shaded sides of a home. The logs were sometimes made from old clothing. These logs could be added as clothing wore out. The foundation they were sewn onto became the inside of the quilt. Battings were not used.

The quilt tops were tied to a backing to add additional warmth. It is believed that they were tied because the different weights of fabric would have made hand quilting impossible.

Today our homes have become more efficient, lighter, and varied in shape and form. And they are stocked with more technology-based items, which makes our day-to-day living a bit easier and brighter.

Log Cabin quilts today are made with wonderful fabrics with bold colors and amazing machines with incredible technology. Why not varied shapes and formations, too? We combined these with a little imagination to get twenty quilts that we believe will appeal to the quilters of today.

The quilts have three size options using 12″ × 12″ blocks—coverlet, throw, and baby.

Think of what type of Log Cabin quilt you want to add to your modern home. Then gather your fabrics, notions, and machine, and you will be ready to begin.

Sewing *basics*

Snowball Corners

Refer to the project instructions for the size of the squares.

1. Lightly draw a diagonal line from a corner to the opposite corner on the wrong side of a smaller square. Place the small square on the corner of a larger square, lining up the outer edges as shown.

2. Sew on the diagonal line from corner to opposite corner on the smaller square. Repeat on all 4 corners.

3. Trim ¼″ beyond stitching. Press triangles toward the corner.

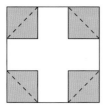

Stitch.

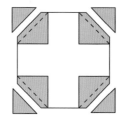

Trim.

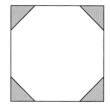

Press.

Half-Square Triangles

No-Waste Method

Refer to the project instructions for the size of the squares.

This method starts with squares that are ⅞″ bigger than the desired finished size. It makes 2 blocks at a time. Suppose you want a finished 3″ half-square triangle. Using this method, you would cut 2 squares 3⅞″ × 3⅞″ and follow these steps.

1. With right sides together, pair 2 squares. Lightly draw a diagonal line from a corner to the opposite corner on the wrong side of the top square.

2. Sew a scant ¼″ seam on each side of the line (Figure A).

3. Cut on the drawn line (Figure B).

4. Press open, and trim off dog-ears (Figure C).

Sew.

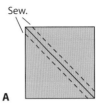

A

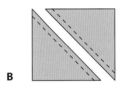

B

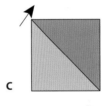

C

Strip Piecing

Strip piecing is a way to sew multiple units quickly. Refer to the project instructions for size information. Cut strips into sections as indicated in the pattern.

For example, many of the patterns in this book start with sewing two squares together. To make multiple units of these two-patch blocks, follow these steps:

1. Cut the strips as directed in the pattern.

2. Place the strips right sides together and sew a ¼˝ seam along a long side.

3. Press the seam toward the darker fabric.

4. Cut the strips into two-patch sections as directed in the pattern.

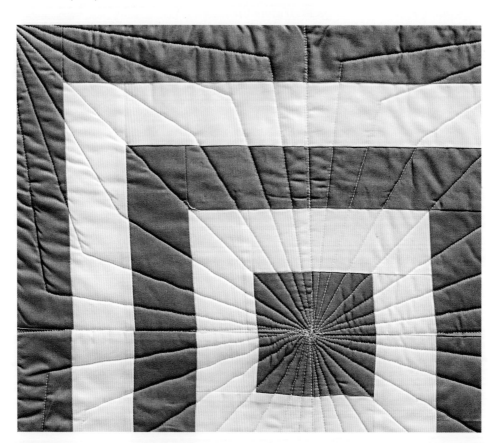

Finishing the Quilt

Backing

Plan on making the backing a minimum of 8″ longer and wider than the quilt top. Piece, if necessary. Trim the selvages before you piece to the desired size.

To economize, piece the back from any leftover quilting fabrics or blocks in your collection.

Batting

The type of batting to use is a personal decision; consult your local quilt shop. Cut batting approximately 8″ longer and wider than the quilt top. Note that your batting choice will affect how much quilting is necessary for the quilt. Check the manufacturer's instructions to see how far apart the quilting lines can be.

Layering

If you are taking your quilt to a longarm quilter, you don't need to layer or baste it.

Spread the backing wrong side up and tape the edges down with masking tape. (If you are working on carpet you can use T-pins to secure the backing to the carpet.) Center the batting on top, smoothing out any folds. Place the quilt top right side up on top of the batting and backing, making sure it is centered.

Basting

Basting keeps the quilt "sandwich" layers from shifting while you are quilting.

If you plan to machine quilt on your domestic machine, pin baste the quilt layers together with safety pins placed about 3″–4″ apart.

Begin pin basting in the center and move toward the edges, first in vertical and then in horizontal rows. Try not to pin directly on the intended quilting lines.

If you plan to hand quilt, baste the layers together with thread using a long needle and light-colored thread. Knot one end of the thread. Using stitches approximately the length of the needle, begin in the center and move out toward the edges in vertical and horizontal rows approximately 4″ apart. Add two diagonal rows of basting.

Quilting

Quilting, whether by hand or machine, enhances the pieced or appliquéd design of the quilt. You may choose to stitch in-the-ditch, echo the pieced or appliquéd motifs, use patterns from quilting design books and stencils, or do your own free-motion quilting. A good guidebook is Natalia's *Beginner's Guide to Free-Motion Quilting* (by C&T Publishing).

Binding

Trim excess batting and backing even with the edges of the quilt top.

Double-Fold Straight-Grain Binding

If you want a ¼″ finished binding, cut the binding strips 2¼″ wide and piece them together with diagonal seams to make a continuous binding strip. Trim the seam allowance to ¼″. Press the seams open. (Figures A & B)

Fold the strip in half lengthwise with the wrong sides together. With raw edges even, pin the binding to the front edge of the quilt a few inches away from the corner, and leave the first few inches of the binding unattached. Start sewing, using a ¼″ seam allowance.

Refer to the drawings (at right). Stop ¼″ away from the first corner (Figure A), and backstitch one stitch. Lift the presser foot and needle. Rotate the quilt one-quarter turn. Fold the binding at a right angle so it extends straight above the quilt and the fold forms a 45° angle in the corner (Figure B). Then bring the binding strip down even with the edge of the quilt (Figure C). Begin sewing at the folded edge. Repeat in the same manner at all corners.

Continue stitching until you are back near the beginning of the binding strip. See Finishing the Binding Ends (page 13) for tips on finishing and hiding the raw edges of the ends of the binding.

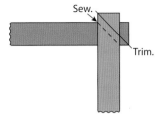

A. Sew from corner to corner.

B. Completed diagonal seam

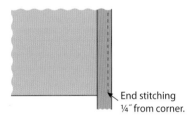

C. Stitch to ¼″ from corner.

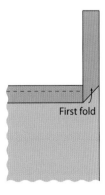

D. First fold for miter

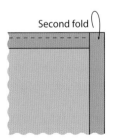

E. Second fold alignment

Continuous Bias Binding

A continuous bias involves using a square sliced in half diagonally and then sewing the triangles together so that you continuously cut marked strips to make a single, long bias strip. The same instructions can be used to cut bias for piping.

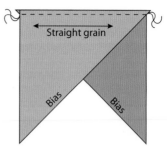

A. Sew triangles together.

> To estimate the size of the square needed, use this formula:
>
> Length of bias strip needed × Width of bias strip = Area of strip
>
> Square root of area of strip = Size of square to be cut

1. Cut the determined fabric square. Then cut the square in half diagonally. Sew the resulting triangles together as shown, using a ¼˝ seam allowance. Press the seam open. (Figure A)

2. Using a ruler, mark the parallelogram created by the 2 triangles with lines spaced the width you need to cut your bias. We cut our lines 2¼˝ apart. Cut about 5˝ along the first line. (Figure B)

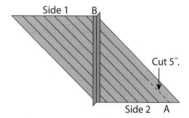

B. Mark lines and begin cutting.

3. Join Side 1 and Side 2 to form a tube. The raw edge at line A will align with the raw edge at B. This will allow the first line to be offset by a strip width. Pin the raw edges right sides together, making sure that the lines match. Sew with a ¼˝ seam allowance. Press the seam open. Cut along the drawn lines, creating a single continuous strip.

C

4. Fold the entire strip in half lengthwise with wrong sides together. Place the binding on the quilt as described in Double-Fold Straight-Grain Binding (page 11).

See Finishing the Binding Ends (page 13) for tips on finishing and hiding the raw edges of the ends of the binding.

Finishing the Binding Ends

METHOD 1

After stitching around the quilt, fold under the beginning tail of the binding strip ¼˝ so that the raw edge will be inside the binding after it is turned to the back side of the quilt. Place the end tail of the binding strip inside the beginning folded end. Continue to attach the binding and stitch slightly beyond the starting stitches. Trim the excess binding. Fold the binding over the raw edges to the quilt back and hand stitch, mitering the corners.

METHOD 2

1. Fold the ending tail of the binding back on itself where it meets the beginning binding tail. From the fold, measure and mark the cut width of the binding strip. Cut the ending binding tail to this measurement. For example, if the binding is cut 2¼˝ wide, measure 2¼˝ from the fold on the ending tail of the binding and cut the binding tail to this length. (Figure D)

2. Open both tails. Place a tail on top of the other tail at right angles, right sides together. Mark a diagonal line from corner to corner and stitch on the line. Check that you've done it correctly and that the binding fits the quilt; then trim the seam allowance to ¼˝. Press open. (Figure E)

3. Refold the binding and stitch this binding section in place on the quilt. Fold the binding over the raw edges to the quilt back and hand stitch.

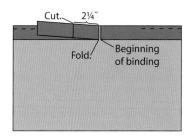

D. Cut binding tail.

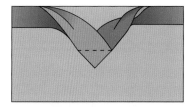

E. Stitch ends of binding diagonally.

Twenty Quilt Designs

Barn Cabins

FINISHED SIZE: 96″ × 96″ • **BLOCK SIZE:** 12″ × 12″

Designed and quilted by Natalia Bonner and Kathleen Whiting; pieced by Ilene Peterson

Quilts that make you think, or take a second look, have become our very favorite types of quilts. Look closely at this quilt and you will see it's made from just one block that has been rotated to give the quilt a cool, modern look. The block is a loose play on the traditional Log Cabin–style quilt block.

Main Quilt Block
Fabric: Michael Miller Fabrics

Alternate Colorway

Materials

Yardages are based on fabric that is at least 40″ wide.

	Baby 36″ × 36″	Throw 60″ × 72″	Coverlet 96″ × 96″
■ Pink fabric	½ yard	1⅛ yards	2⅛ yards
■ Orange fabric	¾ yard	1⅞ yards	3⅞ yards
□ White fabric	1 yard	2½ yards	4⅞ yards
Backing fabric	2½ yards	3⅞ yards	8¾ yards
Binding fabric	⅓ yard	½ yard	¾ yard
Batting	44″ × 44″	68″ × 80″	104″ × 104″

Cutting

	Cut	Baby 9 blocks	Throw 30 blocks	Coverlet 64 blocks
■ From pink fabric	4½″ × 8½″ strips	9	30	64
■ From orange fabric	4½″ × 4½″ squares	9	30	64
	4½″ × 12½″ strips	9	30	64
	2½″ × 2½″ squares	54	180	384
□ From white fabric	4½″ × 4½″ squares	9	30	64
	4½″ × 8½″ strips	9	30	64

Sewing the Block

Seam allowances are ¼˝ unless otherwise indicated. Press block after each step.

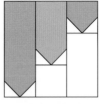

Barn Cabin block

1. Using 2 white 2½˝ squares, make 2 snowball corners (page 6) on a short end of each pink and orange strip. Note the placement of the angles (Figure A). Set long orange units aside until Step 4.

2. Sew a white 4½˝ square to the snowball end of the pink units from Step 1 (Figure B).

3. Sew a white 4½˝ × 8½˝ strip to the snowball end of the short orange units from Step 1 (Figure C).

4. Sew a long orange unit from Step 1 to the left side of a pink unit from Step 2 (Figure D).

5. Referring to the Barn Cabins block diagram, sew an orange unit from Step 3 to the right side of the unit from Step 4 to complete the block.

6. Repeat these steps to make the number of blocks needed (*baby size:* 9 blocks; *throw:* 30 blocks; *coverlet:* 64 blocks).

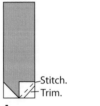
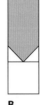

Stitch.
Trim.

A

B

C

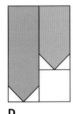

D

Putting It All Together

Refer to the *Barn Cabins* quilt assembly diagram to find the size quilt you are making. Note the block placement; alternate the direction of every other block within each row.

- For the baby size, sew 3 rows of 3 blocks.

- For the throw, sew 6 rows of 5 blocks.

- For the coverlet, sew 8 rows of 8 blocks.

Press the seams in alternating directions from row to row.

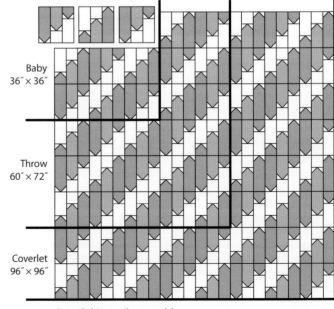

Baby
36˝ × 36˝

Throw
60˝ × 72˝

Coverlet
96˝ × 96˝

Barn Cabins quilt assembly

Finishing

Refer to Finishing the Quilt (page 9) to layer, quilt, and bind the quilt.

Barn Cabins coverlet, 96″ × 96″

Cabin Keys

FINISHED SIZE: 96″ × 96″ • BLOCK SIZE: 12″ × 12″

Designed, pieced, and quilted by Natalia Bonner and Kathleen Whiting

Picture this striking quilt on a boy's bed. I can just imagine my little boy spending hours and hours driving his cars along the stripes! The graphic design is so handsome that it would appeal to a toddler, a tween, or even a grown man.

Materials

Yardages are based on fabric that is at least 40″ wide.

	Baby 36″ × 36″	Throw 60″ × 72″	Coverlet 96″ × 96″
☐ From tan fabric	1⅓ yards	3¼ yards	6⅝ yards
☐ From blue fabric	¾ yard	1¾ yards	4 yards
Backing fabric	2½ yards	3⅞ yards	8¾ yards
Binding fabric	⅓ yard	½ yard	¾ yard
Batting	44″ × 44″	68″ × 80″	104″ × 104″

Cutting

	Cut	Baby 9 blocks	Throw 30 blocks	Coverlet 64 blocks
From tan fabric	2½″ × 2½″ squares	9	30	64
	4½″ × 4½″ strips	9	30	64
	4½″ × 8½″ strips	9	30	64
	2½″ × 10½″ strips	9	30	64
	2½″ × 12½″ strips	9	30	64
From blue fabric	2½″ × 2½″ squares	9	30	64
	2½″ × 4½″ strips	9	30	64
	2½″ × 8½″ strips	9	30	64
	2½″ × 10½″ strips	9	30	64

Main Quilt Block
Fabric: Bella Solids by Moda Fabrics

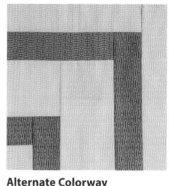

Alternate Colorway

TIP

With some extra planning, you could make Cabin Keys *in multiple colors, with stunning results!*

Sewing the Block

Seam allowances are ¼″ unless otherwise indicated. Press block after each step.

1. Sew a blue 2½″ square to the right side of a tan 2½″ square (Figure A).

2. Sew a blue 2½″ × 4½″ strip to the top of the unit from Step 1 (Figure B).

3. Sew a tan 4½″ square to the right side of the unit and a tan 4½″ × 8½″ strip to the top (Figure C).

4. Sew a blue 2½″ × 8½″ strip to the right side of the unit and a blue 2½″ × 10½″ strip to the top (Figure D).

5. Referring to the Cabin Keys block diagram, sew a tan 2½″ × 10½″ strip to the right side of the unit from Step 4 and a tan 2½″ × 12½″ strip to the top to complete the block.

6. Repeat these steps to make the number of blocks needed (*baby size:* 9 blocks; *throw:* 30 blocks; *coverlet:* 64 blocks).

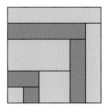

Cabin Keys block

A

B

C

D

Putting It All Together

Refer to the *Cabin Keys* quilt assembly diagram to find the size quilt you are making. Note the block placement; alternate the direction of every other block within each row.

- For the baby size, sew 3 rows of 3 blocks.

- For the throw, sew 6 rows of 5 blocks.

- For the coverlet, sew 8 rows of 8 blocks.

Press the seams in alternating directions from row to row.

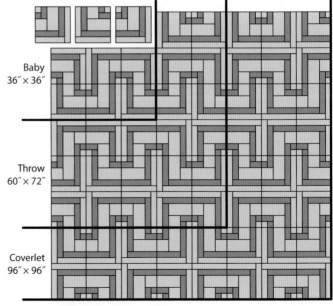

Baby
36″ × 36″

Throw
60″ × 72″

Coverlet
96″ × 96″

Cabin Keys quilt assembly

Finishing

Refer to Finishing the Quilt (page 9) to layer, quilt, and bind the quilt.

Cabin Keys coverlet, 96″ × 96″

Dappled

FINISHED SIZE: 85″ × 85″ • **BLOCK SIZE:** 12″ × 12″

Designed, pieced, and quilted by Natalia Bonner and Kathleen Whiting

It's hard to believe that this intricate design of intersecting squares starts with a very simple Log Cabin quarter-log block!

What are your favorite colors? Pull some from your stash and add some white to make a modern quilt.

Materials

Yardages are based on fabric that is at least 40˝ wide.

	Baby 34˝ × 34˝	Throw 51˝ × 68˝	Coverlet 85˝ × 85˝
Assorted gray fabrics	1 yard	2¼ yards	3¾ yards
White fabric	1⅓ yards	3¼ yards	5½ yards
Backing fabric	2⅓ yards	3⅓ yards	7⅞ yards
Binding fabric	⅓ yard	½ yard	¾ yard
Batting	42˝ × 42˝	59˝ × 76˝	93˝ × 93˝

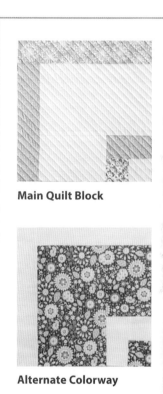

Main Quilt Block

Alternate Colorway

Cutting

	Cut	Baby 12 blocks	Throw 31 blocks	Coverlet 60 blocks
From assorted gray fabrics	2½˝ × 2½˝ squares	12	31	60
	2½˝ × 4½˝ strips	12	31	60
	2½˝ × 10½˝ strips	12	31	60
	2½˝ × 12½˝ strips	12	31	60
From white fabric	2½˝ × 2½˝ squares	12	31	60
	4½˝ × 6½˝ strips	12	31	60
	6½˝ × 10½˝ strips	12	31	60

Sewing the Block

Seam allowances are ¼″ unless otherwise indicated.
Press block after each step.

1. Sew a gray 2½″ square to the right side of a white 2½″ square (Figure A).

2. Sew a gray 2½″ × 4½″ strip to the top of the unit from Step 1 (Figure B).

3. Sew a white 4½″ × 6½″ strip to the right side of the unit and a white 6½″ × 10½″ strip to the top (Figure C).

4. Referring to the Dappled block diagram, sew a gray 2½″ × 10½″ strip to the right side of the unit and a gray 2½″ × 12½″ strip to the top to complete the block.

5. Repeat these steps to make the number of blocks needed (*baby size:* 12 blocks; *throw:* 31 blocks; *coverlet:* 60 blocks).

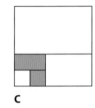

Dappled block

  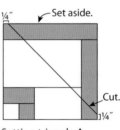

A   B   C

Setting Triangles

Cut blocks in half diagonally ¼″ from the centerline as shown. The small Log Cabin square will be at the center tip of setting triangle A; the plain corner will be at the center tip of setting triangle B.

- For the baby quilt, cut 4 each of setting triangles A and B.

- For the throw, cut 7 each of setting triangles A and B.

- For the coverlet, cut 10 each of setting triangles A and B.

Save the pieces that you cut off; they can be used to make pillows (page 120).

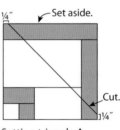

¼″   Set aside.
                                  Cut.
                             1¼″

Setting triangle A

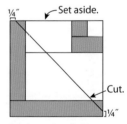

¼″   Set aside.
                                  Cut.
                             1¼″

Setting triangle B

Putting It All Together

Refer to the *Dappled* quilt assembly diagram for the size quilt you are making. Arrange the blocks and setting triangles in diagonal rows. Note the block placement; alternate the direction of every other block in each row. Also alternate the setting triangles.

- For the baby size, use 4 blocks and 8 setting triangles.

- For the throw, use 17 blocks and 14 setting triangles.

- For the coverlet, use 40 blocks and 20 setting triangles.

Press the seams in alternating directions from row to row.

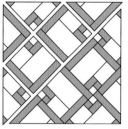

Dappled baby quilt assembly, finished 34˝ × 34˝

Dappled throw quilt assembly, finished 51˝ × 68˝

Dappled coverlet quilt assembly, finished 85˝ × 85˝

Finishing

Refer to Finishing the Quilt (page 9) to layer, quilt, and bind the quilt.

Dappled coverlet, 85″ × 85″

Dazzle

FINISHED SIZE: 96″ × 96″ • **BLOCK SIZE:** 12″ × 12″

Designed, pieced, and quilted by Natalia Bonner and Kathleen Whiting

Pull your favorite scraps or use an interesting fat quarter bundle to make this fabulous quilt. Fabric choice is key; be sure there is a lot of contrast between the dark and light fabrics to really make the pattern pop!

Materials

Yardages are based on fabric that is at least 40″ wide.

	Baby 36″ × 36″	Throw 60″ × 72″	Coverlet 96″ × 96″
■ Dark fabric	1½ yards	3 yards	5¾ yards
□ Light fabric	¾ yard	1¼ yards	2⅜ yards
□ White fabric	¾ yard	2¼ yards	4¾ yards
Backing fabric	2½ yards	3⅞ yards	8¾ yards
Binding fabric	⅓ yard	½ yard	¾ yard
Batting	44″ × 44″	68″ × 80″	104″ × 104″

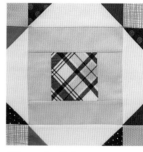

Main Quilt Block
Fabric: Simply Style by Vanessa Christenson for Moda Fabrics

Alternate Colorway

Cutting

	Cut	Baby 9 blocks	Throw 30 blocks	Coverlet 64 blocks
From assorted dark-value fabrics ■	2½″ × 2½″ squares	72	240	512
	Cut a pair of 2½″ × 4½″ strips and a pair of 2½″ × 8½″ strips from the same fabric for each block:			
	2½″ × 4½″ strips	18	60	128
	2½″ × 8½″ strips	18	60	128
From light-value fabric □	4½″ × 4½″ squares	9	30	64
	2½″ × 2½″ squares	36	120	256
From white fabric □	2½″ × 8½″ strips	36	120	256

Sewing the Block

Seam allowances are ¼″ unless otherwise indicated. Press after each step.

1. Using 2 dark 2½″ squares, make a snowball corner (page 6) on each end of a white 2½″ × 8½″ strip. Note placement of the angles (Figure A).

Make 4. Set 2 aside.

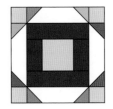

Dazzle block

2. Sew a light 2½″ square to each end of 2 of the units from Step 1 (Figure B).

Set aside.

3. Sew 2 matching-color dark 2½″ × 4½″ strips to opposite sides of a light 4½″ square. Sew 2 dark 2½″ × 8½″ strips in the same color to the top and bottom (Figure C).

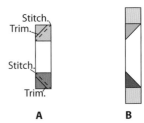

4. Sew 2 units from Step 1 to the top and bottom of the unit from Step 3 (Figure D).

5. Referring to the Dazzle block diagram, sew 2 units from Step 2 to opposite sides of the unit from Step 4 to complete the block.

6. Repeat these steps to make the number of blocks needed (*baby size:* 9 blocks; *throw:* 30 blocks; *coverlet:* 64 blocks).

Putting It All Together

Refer to the *Dazzle* quilt assembly diagram to find the size quilt you are making. Alternate the block color in every other block.

- For the baby size, sew 3 rows of 3 blocks.

- For the throw, sew 6 rows of 5 blocks.

- For the coverlet, sew 8 rows of 8 blocks.

Press the seams in alternating directions from row to row.

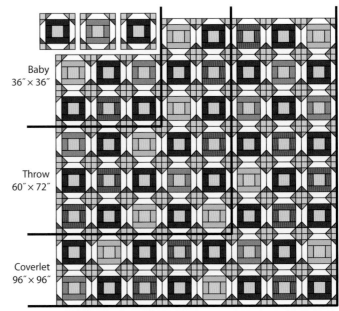

Baby
36″ × 36″

Throw
60″ × 72″

Coverlet
96″ × 96″

Dazzle quilt assembly

Finishing

Refer to Finishing the Quilt (page 9) to layer, quilt, and bind the quilt.

Dazzle coverlet, 96″ × 96″

Dilation

FINISHED SIZE: 96″ × 96″ • **BLOCK SIZE:** 12″ × 12″

Designed, pieced, and quilted by Natalia Bonner and Kathleen Whiting

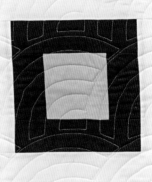

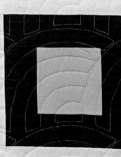

This fun twist on a Log Cabin is simple yet stunning. Its large pieces and simple construction make it a great pattern for a beginning quiltmaker.

Materials

Yardages are based on fabric that is at least 40″ wide.

	Baby 36″ × 36″	Throw 60″ × 72″	Coverlet 96″ × 96″
Mustard fabric	¼ yard	⅝ yard	1¼ yards
Plum fabric	½ yard	1½ yards	3⅜ yards
White fabric	1 yard	2⅞ yards	5¾ yards
Backing fabric	2½ yards	3⅞ yards	8¾ yards
Binding fabric	⅓ yard	½ yard	¾ yard
Batting	44″ × 44″	68″ × 80″	104″ × 104″

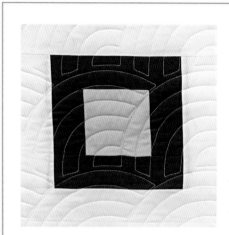

Main Quilt Block
Fabric: Bella Solids by Moda Fabrics

Alternate Colorway

Cutting

	Cut	Baby 9 blocks	Throw 30 blocks	Coverlet 64 blocks
From mustard fabric	2½″ × 2½″ squares	9	15	24
	4½″ × 4½″ squares		15	24
	6½″ × 6½″ squares			16
From plum fabric	2½″ × 2½″ squares	18	30	48
	2½″ × 4½″ strips		30	48
	2½″ × 6½″ strips	18	30	80
	2½″ × 8½″ strips		30	48
	2½″ × 10½″ strips			32
	3½″ × 6½″ strips	18	30	48
	3½″ × 12½″ strips	18	30	48
From white fabric	2½″ × 8½″ strips		30	48
	2½″ × 12½″ strips		30	48
	1½″ × 10½″ strips			32
	1½″ × 12½″ strips			32

Sewing the Blocks

Seam allowances are ¼″ unless otherwise indicated. Press after each step.

Small Block

1. Sew 2 plum 2½″ squares to opposite sides of a mustard 2½″ square (Figure A).

2. Sew 2 plum 2½″ × 6½″ strips to the top and bottom of the unit (Figure B).

3. Referring to the Dilation small block diagram, sew 2 white 3½″ × 6½″ strips to opposite sides of the unit and 2 white 3½″ × 12½″ strips to the top and bottom to complete the block.

4. Repeat these steps to make the number of blocks needed (*baby size:* 9 blocks; *throw:* 15 blocks; *coverlet:* 24 blocks).

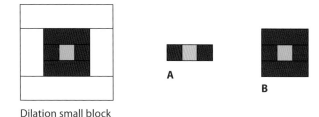

Dilation small block

A

B

Medium Block

This block is needed for the throw and coverlet sizes only.

1. Sew 2 plum 2½″ × 4½″ strips to opposite sides of a mustard 4½″ square (Figure C).

2. Sew 2 plum 2½″ × 8½″ strips to the top and bottom of the unit (Figure D).

3. Referring to the Dilation medium block diagram, sew 2 white 2½″ × 8½″ strips to opposite sides of the unit and 2 white 2½″ × 12½″ strips to the top and bottom to complete the block.

4. Repeat these steps to make the number of blocks needed (*throw:* 15 blocks; *coverlet:* 24 blocks).

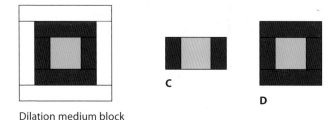

Dilation medium block

C

D

Large Block

This block is needed for the coverlet size only.

1. Sew 2 plum 2½″ × 6½″ strips to opposite sides of a mustard 6½″ square (Figure E).

2. Sew 2 plum 2½″ × 10½″ strips to the top and bottom of the unit (Figure F).

3. Referring to the Dilation large block diagram, sew 2 white 1½″ × 10½″ strips to opposite sides of the unit and 2 white 1½″ × 12½″ strips to the top and bottom to complete the block.

4. Repeat these steps to make 16 blocks for the coverlet size.

Dilation large block

E

F

Putting It All Together

Refer to the *Dilation* quilt assembly diagram to find the size quilt you are making. Note the block placement to arrange the small, medium, and large blocks correctly.

- For the baby size, sew 3 rows of 3 blocks.

- For the throw, sew 6 rows of 5 blocks.

- For the coverlet, sew 8 rows of 8 blocks.

Press the seams in alternating directions from row to row.

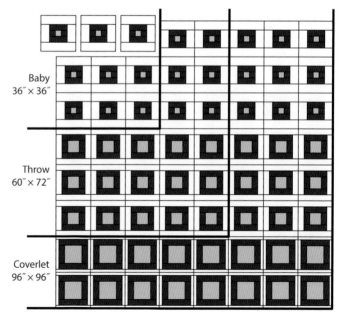

Dilation quilt assembly, finished 96″ × 96″

Finishing

Refer to Finishing the Quilt (page 9) to layer, quilt, and bind the quilt.

Dilation coverlet, 96″ × 96″

Downtown Cabins

FINISHED SIZE: 85″ × 85″ • **BLOCK SIZE:** 12″ × 12″

Designed, pieced, and quilted by Natalia Bonner and Kathleen Whiting

Grab a few of your favorite solid colors, cut your strips, and begin sewing! This quilt is made from large pieces, so it sews together quickly. Great quilt for a beginner. To really spice this quilt up, you could mix in some of your favorite prints.

Materials

Yardages are based on fabric that is at least 40″ wide.

	Baby 34″ × 34″	Throw 68″ × 68″	Coverlet 85″ × 85″
☐ Light gray fabric	½ yard	1½ yards	2⅛ yards
☐ White fabric	⅔ yard	2⅛ yards	3 yards
☐ Yellow fabric	½ yard	¾ yard	1⅛ yards
■ Pink fabric	½ yard	¾ yard	1⅛ yards
☐ Blue fabric	½ yard	¾ yard	1⅛ yards
☐ Orange fabric	½ yard	¾ yard	1⅛ yards
☐ Dark gray fabric	⅓ yard	¾ yard	1 yard
Backing fabric	2⅓ yards	4¼ yards	7¾ yards
Binding fabric	⅓ yard	⅝ yard	¾ yard
Batting	42″ × 42″	76″ × 76″	93″ × 93″

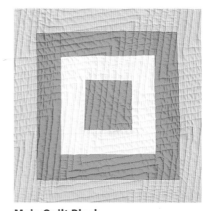

Main Quilt Block
Fabric: Bella Solids by Moda Fabrics and Cotton Couture by Michael Miller Fabrics

Alternate Colorway

Cutting

	Cut	Baby 12 blocks	Throw 40 blocks	Coverlet 60 blocks
From light gray fabric	2″ × 9½″ strips	12	40	60
	2″ × 12½″ strips	12	40	60
From white fabric	2″ × 9½″ strips	12	40	60
	2″ × 12½″ strips	12	40	60
	2″ × 3½″ strips	12	40	60
	2″ × 6½″ strips	12	40	60
From each: yellow, pink, blue, and orange fabric	3½″ × 3½″ squares	3	10	15
	2″ × 6½″ strips	6	20	30
	2″ × 9½″ strips	6	20	30
From dark gray fabric	2″ × 3½″ strips	12	40	60
	2″ × 6½″ strips	12	40	60

Sewing the Blocks

Seam allowances are ¼″ unless otherwise indicated. Press after each step.

Block A: Yellow and Pink

The construction for these two blocks is the same. Use the following instructions and yellow or pink pieces to make either block.

1. Sew 2 dark gray 2″ × 3½″ strips to opposite sides of a 3½″ color square (Figure A).

2. Sew 2 dark gray 2″ × 6½″ strips to the top and bottom (Figure B).

3. Sew 2 color 2″ × 6½″ strips to opposite sides of the unit and 2 color 2″ × 9½″ strips to the top and bottom (Figure C).

4. Referring to the Downtown Cabins block A diagrams, sew 2 white 2″ × 9½″ strips to opposite sides of the unit and 2 white 2″ × 12½″ strips to the top and bottom to complete the block.

5. Repeat these steps to make the number of blocks needed in both yellow and pink (*baby size:* 3 blocks each; *throw:* 10 blocks each; *coverlet:* 15 blocks each).

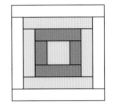

Yellow Downtown
Cabins block

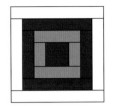

Pink Downtown
Cabins block

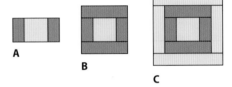

A B C

Block B: Orange and Blue

The construction for these two blocks is the same. Use the following instructions and orange or blue pieces to make either block.

1. Sew 2 white 2″ × 3½″ strips to opposite sides of a color 3½″ square (Figure D).

2. Sew 2 white 2″ × 6½″ strips to the top and bottom (Figure E).

3. Sew 2 color 2″ × 6½″ strips to opposite sides of the unit and 2 color 2″ × 9½″ strips to the top and bottom (Figure F).

4. Referring to the Downtown Cabins block B diagrams, sew 2 light gray 2″ × 9½″ strips to opposite sides of the unit and 2 light gray 2″ × 12½″ strips to the top and bottom to complete the block.

5. Repeat these steps to make the number of blocks needed in both orange and blue (*baby size:* 3 blocks each; *throw:* 10 blocks each; *coverlet:* 15 blocks each).

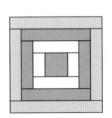

Orange Downtown
Cabins block

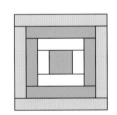

Blue Downtown
Cabins block

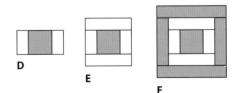

D E F

Setting Triangles

Cut blocks in half diagonally ¼″ from the centerline as shown (Figure G). *Don't throw away the halves that you cut off. They can be used to make pillows (page 120).*

- For the baby size, cut 2 setting triangles in each color, 8 total.

- For the throw size, cut 4 setting triangles from each color, 16 total.

- For the coverlet size, cut 5 setting triangles from each color, 20 total.

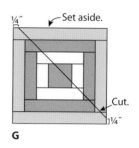

G

Putting It All Together

Refer to the *Downtown Cabins* quilt assembly diagram for the size quilt you are making. Arrange the blocks and setting triangles in diagonal rows.

- For the baby size, use 4 blocks and 8 setting triangles.

- For the throw, use 24 blocks and 16 setting triangles.

- For the coverlet, use 40 blocks and 20 setting triangles.

Press the seams in alternating directions from row to row.

Downtown Cabins baby quilt assembly, finished 34″ × 34″

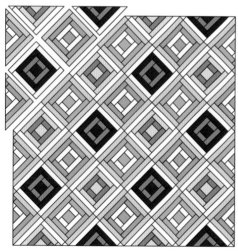

Downtown Cabins throw quilt assembly, finished 68″ × 68″

Downtown Cabins coverlet quilt assembly, finished 85″ × 85″

Finishing

Refer to Finishing the Quilt (page 9) to layer, quilt, and bind the quilt.

Downtown Cabins coverlet, 85″ × 85″

Floating Cabins

FINISHED SIZE: 96″ × 96″ • **BLOCK SIZE:** 12″ × 12″

Designed, pieced, and quilted by Natalia Bonner and Kathleen Whiting

Grab a few of your favorite solid colors, cut your strips, and begin sewing! This quilt is made from large pieces, so it sews together quickly. The block arrangement in this quilt creates a secondary block with a framed-square look. This would be an easy yet interesting quilt for a beginner.

Materials

Yardages are based on fabric that is at least 40″ wide.

	Baby 36″ × 36″	Throw 60″ × 72″	Coverlet 96″ × 96″
☐ Sand fabric	⅝ yard	1⅝ yards	3¼ yards
☐ Pistachio fabric	⅜ yard	¾ yard	1⅜ yards
☐ Orange fabric	½ yard	1⅛ yards	2⅛ yards
☐ Stone fabric	¼ yard	⅜ yard	⅝ yard
☐ Ivory fabric	⅝ yard	1⅞ yards	3¾ yards
Backing fabric	2½ yards	3⅞ yards	8¾ yards
Binding fabric	⅓ yard	½ yard	¾ yard
Batting	44″ × 44″	68″ × 80″	104″ × 104″

Main Quilt Block
Fabric: Bella Solids by Moda Fabrics

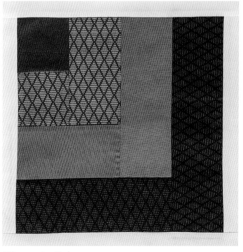

Alternate Colorway

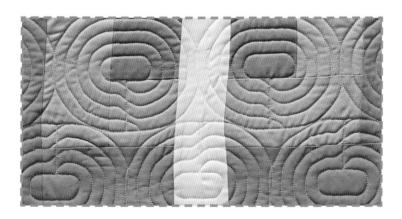

Cutting

	Cut	Baby 9 blocks	Throw 30 blocks	Coverlet 64 blocks
☐ **From stone fabric**	3″ × 3″ squares	9	30	64
☐ **From pistachio fabric**	3″ × 3″ squares	9	30	64
	3″ × 5½″ strips	9	30	64
☐ **From orange fabric**	3″ × 5½″ squares	9	30	64
	3″ × 8″ strips	9	30	64
☐ **From sand fabric**	3″ × 8″ squares	9	30	64
	3″ × 10½″ strips	9	30	64
☐ **From ivory fabric**	1½″ × 10½″ squares	18	60	128
	1½″ × 12½″ strips	18	60	128

Sewing the Block

Seam allowances are ¼″ unless otherwise indicated. Press after each step.

1. Sew a pistachio 3″ square to the left side of a stone 3″ square (Figure A).

2. Sew a pistachio 3″ × 5½″ strip to the top of the unit from Step 1 (Figure B).

3. Sew an orange 3″ × 5½″ strip to the left side of the unit and an orange 3″ × 8″ strip to the top (Figure C).

4. Sew a sand 3″ × 8″ strip to the left side of the unit and a sand 3″ × 10½″ strip to the top (Figure D).

5. Referring to the Floating Cabins block diagram, sew 2 ivory 1½″ × 10½″ strips to the opposite sides of the unit and 2 ivory 1½″ × 12½″ strips to the top and bottom to complete the block.

6. Repeat these steps to make the number of blocks needed (*baby size:* 9 blocks; *throw:* 30 blocks; *coverlet:* 64 blocks).

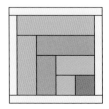

Floating Cabins block

A

B

C

D

Putting It All Together

Refer to the *Floating Cabins* quilt assembly diagram to find the size quilt you are making. Note the block placement and alternate the direction of every other block within each row.

- For the baby size, sew 3 rows of 3 blocks.

- For the throw, sew 6 rows of 5 blocks.

- For the coverlet, sew 8 rows of 8 blocks.

Press the seams in alternating directions from row to row.

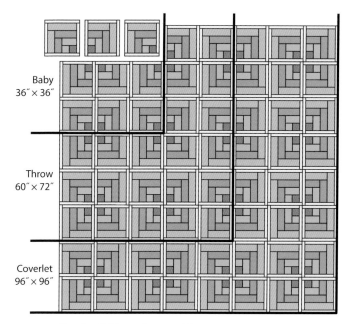

Floating Cabins quilt assembly

Finishing

Refer to Finishing the Quilt (page 9) to layer, quilt, and bind the quilt.

Floating Cabins coverlet, 96″ × 96″

Framed Cabins

FINISHED SIZE: 96″ × 96″ • BLOCK SIZE: 12″ × 12″

Designed, pieced, and quilted by Natalia Bonner and Kathleen Whiting

Grab a few of your favorite solid colors, cut your strips, and begin sewing. This quilt sews together quickly! With its large solid-color pieces, this would be a fun quilt to show off your machine quilting, but it would be equally interesting if you featured your favorite big-scale prints in the large open areas.

Materials

Yardages are based on fabric that is at least 40″ wide.

	Baby 36″ × 36″	Throw 60″ × 72″	Coverlet 96″ × 96″
☐ Green fabric	⅜ yard	⅞ yard	1¾ yards
☐ Blue fabric	⅜ yard	1 yard	2 yards
☐ White fabric	1¼ yards	3¼ yards	6⅞ yards
Backing fabric	2½ yards	3⅞ yards	8¾ yards
Binding fabric	⅓ yard	½ yard	¾ yard
Batting	44″ × 44″	68″ × 80″	104″ × 104″

Main Quilt Block
Fabric: Bella Solids by Moda Fabrics and prints from Michael Miller Fabrics

Cutting

	Cut	Baby 9 blocks	Throw 30 blocks	Coverlet 64 blocks
☐ From green fabric	2½″ × 12½″ squares	9	30	64
☐ From blue fabric	2½″ × 10½″ strips	9	30	64
	2½″ × 2½″ squares	9	30	64
☐ From white fabric	10½″ × 10½″ squares	9	30	64

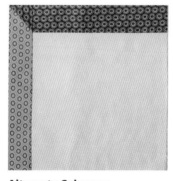

Alternate Colorway

Sewing the Block

Seam allowances are ¼″ unless otherwise indicated. Press after each step.

1. Use a blue 2½″ square to make a snowball corner (page 6) on an end of a green 2½″ × 12½″ strip. Note the angle of the diagonal. Set aside (Figure A).

2. Sew a blue 2½″ × 10½″ strip to the right side of a white 10½″ square (Figure B).

3. Referring to the Framed Cabins block diagram, sew the unit from Step 1 to the top of the unit from Step 2 to complete the block.

4. Repeat these steps to make the number of blocks needed (*baby size:* 9 blocks; *throw:* 30 blocks; *coverlet:* 64 blocks).

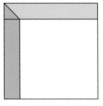

Framed Cabins block

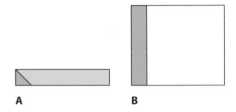

A   B

Putting It All Together

Refer to the *Framed Cabins* quilt assembly diagram to find the size quilt you are making. Note the block placement and alternate the direction of every other block in each row.

- For the baby size, sew 3 rows of 3 blocks.

- For the throw, sew 6 rows of 5 blocks.

- For the coverlet, sew 8 rows of 8 blocks.

Press the seams in alternating directions from row to row.

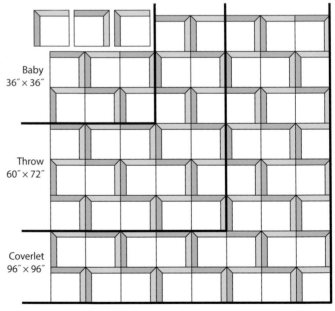

Baby
36″ × 36″

Throw
60″ × 72″

Coverlet
96″ × 96″

Framed Cabins quilt assembly

Finishing

Refer to Finishing the Quilt (page 9) to layer, quilt, and bind the quilt.

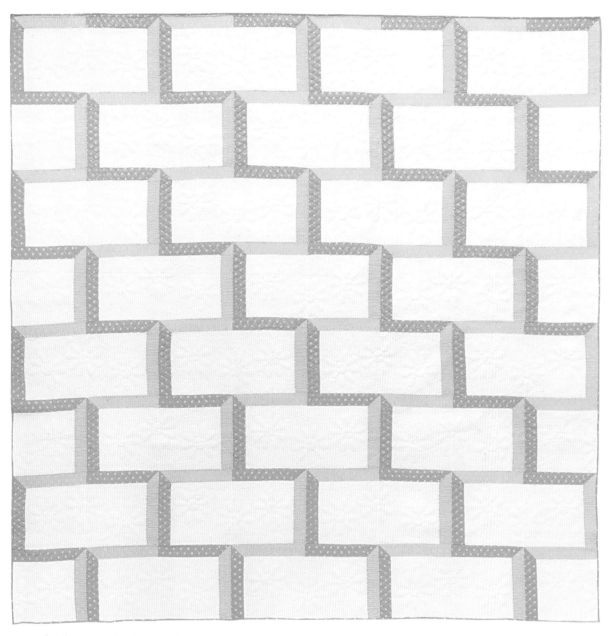

Framed Cabins coverlet, 96˝ × 96˝

Incline

FINISHED SIZE: 96″ × 96″ • **BLOCK SIZE:** 12″ × 12″

Designed, pieced, and quilted by Natalia Bonner and Kathleen Whiting

Grab three print jelly rolls in your favorite colors and four solid white jelly rolls, and then add little bit of solid white fabric. You'll be almost ready to sew!

Materials

Yardages are based on fabric that is at least 40˝ wide.

	Baby 36˝ × 36˝	Throw 60˝ × 72˝	Coverlet 96˝ × 96˝
■ Assorted fabric	⅝ yard	1⅔ yards	3⅜ yards
□ White fabric	1⅜ yards	3½ yards	6¾ yards
Backing fabric	2½ yards	3⅞ yards	8¾ yards
Binding fabric	⅓ yard	½ yard	¾ yard
Batting	44˝ × 44˝	68˝ × 80˝	104˝ × 104˝

Main Quilt Block
Fabric: Simply Style by Vanessa Christenson for Moda Fabrics

Alternate Colorway

Cutting

To create the look of overlapping squares in different colors as shown in the coverlet (page 59), make sets of 2 or 3 blocks in matching colors for each square. For this look in the baby quilt, you would need 2 sets of 2 blocks and 2 singles (6 blocks total). For the throw, you would need 3 sets of 2 blocks, 5 sets of 3 blocks, and 2 singles (23 blocks total). For the coverlet, you will need 4 sets of 2 blocks, 12 sets of 3 blocks, and 4 singles (48 blocks total).

	Cut	Baby 9 blocks	Throw 30 blocks	Coverlet 64 blocks
	To make a matching pair of blocks, cut 2 print strips of each length in the same fabric. *For a matching set of 3 blocks, cut 3 strips in the same fabric.*			
◼ **From assorted print fabrics**	2½″ × 2½″ squares	6	23	48
	2½″ × 4½″ strips	6	23	48
	2½″ × 6½″ strips	6	23	48
	2½″ × 8½″ strips	6	23	48
	2½″ × 10½″ strips	6	23	48
◻ **From white fabric**	2½″ × 2½″ squares	6	23	48
	2½″ × 4½″ strips	6	23	48
	2½″ × 6½″ strips	6	23	48
	2½″ × 8½″ strips	6	23	48
	2½″ × 10½″ strips	6	23	48
	2½″ × 12½″ strips	6	23	48
	12½″ × 12½″ squares	3	7	16

Sewing the Block

Use matching print fabric throughout each block. Seam allowances are ¼˝ unless otherwise indicated. Press after each step.

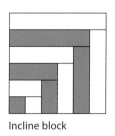

Incline block

1. Sew a white 2½˝ square to the right side of a print 2½˝ square (Figure A).

2. Sew a white 2½˝ × 4½˝ strip to the top of the unit from Step 1 (Figure B).

3. Sew a print 2½˝ × 4½˝ strip to the right side of the unit and a print 2½˝ × 6½˝ strip to the top (Figure C).

4. Sew a white 2½˝ × 6½˝ strip to the right side of the unit and a white 2½˝ × 8½˝ strip to the top (Figure D).

A   B   C

5. Sew a print 2½˝ × 8½˝ strip to the right side of the unit and a print 2½˝ × 10½˝ strip to the top (Figure E).

6. Referring to the Incline block diagram, sew a white 2½˝ × 10½˝ strip to the right side of the unit and a white 2½˝ × 12½˝ strip to the top to complete the block.

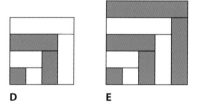

D   E

7. Repeat these steps to make the number of blocks needed (*baby size:* 6 blocks; *throw:* 23 blocks; *coverlet:* 48 blocks).

Putting It All Together

Refer to the *Incline* quilt assembly diagram for the size quilt you are making. Note the block and color placement. Alternate the direction of the block and add white 12½˝ squares to create the design as shown.

- For the baby size, use 6 blocks and 3 white 12½˝ squares. Sew 3 rows of 3 blocks.

- For the throw, use 23 blocks and 7 white 12½˝ squares. Sew 6 rows of 5 blocks.

- For the coverlet, use 48 blocks and 16 white 12½˝ squares. Sew 8 rows of 8 blocks.

Press the seams in alternating directions from row to row.

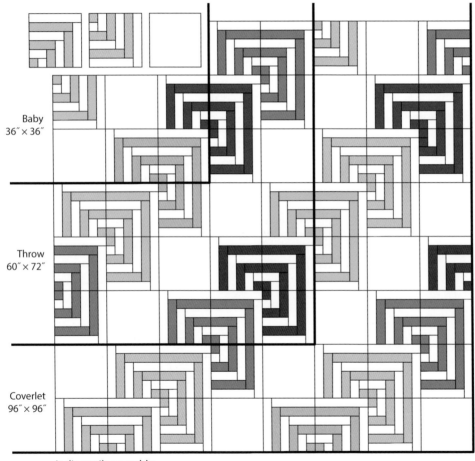

Baby
36˝ × 36˝

Throw
60˝ × 72˝

Coverlet
96˝ × 96˝

Incline quilt assembly

Finishing

Refer to Finishing the Quilt (page 9) to layer, quilt, and bind the quilt.

Incline coverlet, 96″ × 96″

Jawbreaker

FINISHED SIZE: 96″ × 96″ • **BLOCK SIZE:** 12″ × 12″

Designed, pieced, and quilted by Natalia Bonner and Kathleen Whiting

Looking for something fresh, simple, and modern? Jawbreaker is just that. In our modern version, offset squares in six bright colors surround yummy bright yellow centers. For a softer look, try prints to complement your decor.

Materials

Yardages are based on fabric that is at least 40″ wide.

	Baby 36″ × 36″	Throw 60″ × 72″	Coverlet 96″ × 96″
Light pink, dark pink, light blue, and dark blue fabrics	¼ yard each	½ yard each	¾ yard each
Dark green and light green fabrics	¼ yard each	½ yard each	¾ yard each
Yellow fabric	¼ yard	⅓ yard	¾ yard
White fabric	1 yard	2⅝ yards	5⅝ yards
Backing fabric	2½ yards	3⅞ yards	8¾ yards
Binding fabric	⅓ yard	½ yard	¾ yard
Batting	44″ × 44″	68″ × 80″	104″ × 104″

Main Quilt Block
Fabric: Cotton Couture by Michael Miller Fabrics

Alternate Colorway

TIP

This quilt would be a great use of fat quarters.

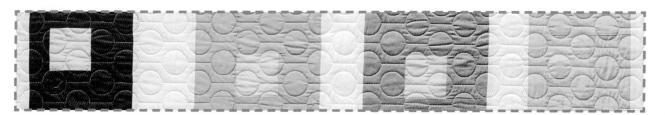

Cutting

	Cut	Baby 9 blocks	Throw 30 blocks	Coverlet 64 blocks
■ ■ □ ■ **From light pink, dark pink, light blue, and dark blue fabrics**	3½" × 3½" squares	1 each of blues, 2 each of pinks (6 total)	5 of each	11 of each
	2" × 9½" strips	1 each of blues, 2 each of pinks (6 total)	5 of each	11 of each
	3½" × 6½" strips	2 each of blues, 4 each of pinks (12 total)	10 of each	22 of each
■ □ **From light green and dark green fabrics**	3½" × 3½" squares	2 light green, 1 dark green	5 of each	10 of each
	2" × 9½" strips	2 light green, 1 dark green	5 of each	10 of each
	3½" × 6½" strips	4 light green, 2 dark green	10 of each	20 of each
□ **From yellow fabric**	3½" × 3½" squares	9	30	64
	2" × 8" strips	9	30	64
□ **From white fabric**	3½" × 11" strips	9	30	64
	2" × 11" strips	9	30	64
	2" × 12½" strips	9	30	64

Sewing the Block

Seam allowances are ¼" unless otherwise indicated. Press block after each step.

1. Sew a color 3½" square to the right side of a yellow 3½" square (Figure A).

2. Sew a matching color 3½" × 6½" strip to the top of the unit from Step 1 (Figure B).

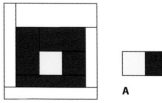

A   B

Jawbreaker block

3. Sew a matching color 3½″ × 6½″ strip to the left side of the unit and a matching color 2″ × 9½″ strip to the bottom (Figure C).

4. Sew a white 2″ × 8″ strip to the right side of the unit and a white 3½″ × 11″ strip to the top (Figure D).

5. Referring to the Jawbreaker block diagram, sew a white 2″ × 11″ strip to the left side of the unit and a white 2″ × 12½″ strip to the bottom to complete the block.

6. Repeat these steps to make the number of blocks needed (*baby size:* 9 blocks; *throw:* 30 blocks; *coverlet:* 64 blocks).

Putting It All Together

Refer to the *Jawbreaker* quilt assembly diagram to find the size quilt you are making. Note the block placement and rotate the blocks within the rows.

- For the baby size, sew 3 rows of 3 blocks.

- For the throw, sew 6 rows of 5 blocks.

- For the coverlet, sew 8 rows of 8 blocks.

Press the seams in alternating directions from row to row.

Finishing

Refer to Finishing the Quilt (page 9) to layer, quilt, and bind the quilt.

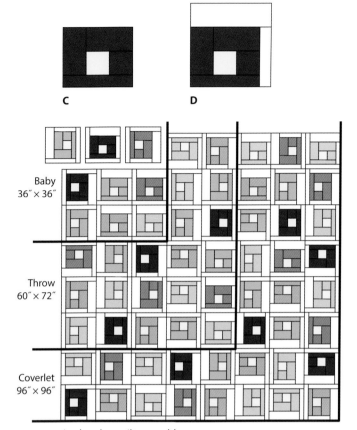

C   D

Baby
36″ × 36″

Throw
60″ × 72″

Coverlet
96″ × 96″

Jawbreaker quilt assembly

Jawbreaker coverlet, 96″ × 96″

Math Class Cabins

FINISHED SIZE: 96″ × 96″ • **BLOCK SIZE:** 12″ × 12″

Designed, pieced, and quilted by Natalia Bonner and Kathleen Whiting

Grab your stash, a couple of jelly rolls, or a bundle of Art Gallery Oval Elements, and have fun making this simple yet bold version of a modern Log Cabin quilt. This quilt features 2½″ strips, so it would be the perfect quilt for a solid-colored jelly roll combined with a couple of print jelly rolls.

Materials

Yardages are based on fabric that is at least 40″ wide.

	Baby 36″ × 36″	Throw 60″ × 72″	Coverlet 96″ × 96″
◼ Assorted fabric	1 yard	2¼ yards	4½ yards
◻ White fabric	1⅛ yards	2⅞ yards	6 yards
Backing fabric	2½ yards	3⅞ yards	8¾ yards
Binding fabric	⅓ yard	½ yard	¾ yard
Batting	44″ × 44″	68″ × 80″	104″ × 104″

TIP

This quilt would be a great quilt to use up your stash or a few print and solid-colored jelly rolls.

Main Quilt Block
Fabric: Oval Elements by Art Gallery Fabrics

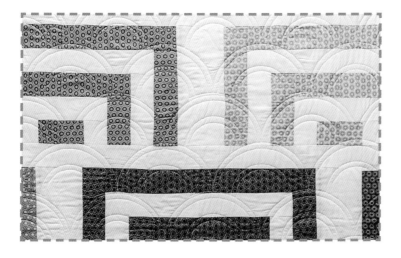

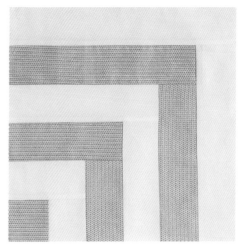

Alternate Colorway

Cutting

To create this design, make some blocks in matching colors. For the baby quilt, you will need 3 pairs of blocks and 3 singles (9 blocks total). For the throw, you will need 12 pairs of blocks and 6 singles (30 blocks total). For the coverlet, you will need 28 pairs of blocks and 8 singles (64 blocks total).

To make a matching pair of blocks, cut 2 strips of each size in matching fabric.

	Cut	Baby 9 blocks	Throw 30 blocks	Coverlet 64 blocks
	To make a matching pair of blocks, cut 2 print strips of each length in the same fabric.			
From assorted fabrics	2½" × 2½" squares	9	30	64
	2½" × 4½" strips	9	30	64
	2½" × 6½" strips	9	30	64
	2½" × 8½" strips	9	30	64
	2½" × 10½" strips	9	30	64
From white fabric	2½" × 2½" squares	9	30	64
	2½" × 4½" strips	9	30	64
	2½" × 6½" strips	9	30	64
	2½" × 8½" strips	9	30	64
	2½" × 10½" strips	9	30	64
	2½" × 12½" strips	9	30	64

Sewing the Block

Seam allowances are ¼″ unless otherwise indicated. Press after every step.

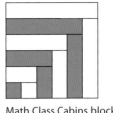

Math Class Cabins block

1. Sew a white 2½″ square to the right side of a print 2½″ × 2½″ square (Figure A).

2. Sew a white 2½″ × 4½″ strip to the top of the unit from Step 1 (Figure B).

3. Sew a print 2½″ × 4½″ strip to the right side of the unit and a print 2½″ × 6½″ strip to the top (Figure C).

4. Sew a white 2½″ × 6½″ strip to the right side of the unit and a white 2½″ × 8½″ strip to the top (Figure D).

5. Sew a print 2½″ × 8½″ strip to the right side of the unit and a print 2½″ × 10½″ strip to the top (Figure E).

6. Referring to the Math Class Cabins block diagram, sew a white 2½″ × 10½″ strip to the right side of the unit and a white 2½″ × 12½″ strip to the top to complete the block.

7. Repeat these steps to make the number of blocks needed (*baby size:* 9 blocks including 3 pairs; *throw:* 30 blocks including 12 pairs; *coverlet:* 64 blocks including 28 pairs).

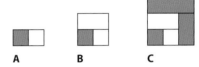

A   B   C

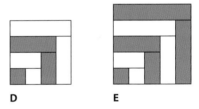

D   E

Putting It All Together

Refer to the *Math Class Cabins* quilt assembly diagram to find the size quilt you are making. Note the block placement and alternate the direction of every other block within the rows. Start the odd rows with a matching pair of blocks; start the even rows with a single block.

- For the baby size, sew 3 rows of 3 blocks.

- For the throw, sew 6 rows of 5 blocks.

- For the coverlet, sew 8 rows of 8 blocks.

Press the seams in alternating directions from row to row.

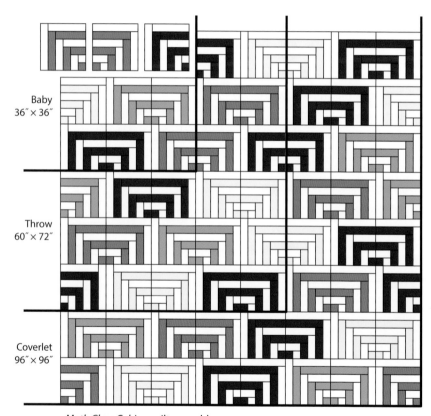

Baby
36″ × 36″

Throw
60″ × 72″

Coverlet
96″ × 96″

Math Class Cabins quilt assembly

Finishing

Refer to Finishing the Quilt (page 9) to layer, quilt, and bind the quilt.

Math Class Cabins coverlet, 96″ × 96″

Metropolis

FINISHED SIZE: 96″ × 96″ • **BLOCK SIZE:** 12″ × 12″

Designed, pieced, and quilted by Natalia Bonner and Kathleen Whiting

Metropolis is a fun way to show off your favorite solid-color fabrics.

This also could be a beautiful Americana quilt in more traditional reds, whites, and blues.

Materials

Yardages are based on fabric that is at least 40″ wide.

	Baby 36″ × 36″	Throw 60″ × 72″	Coverlet 96″ × 96″
Gray fabric	1 yard	2¼ yards	4½ yards
Red fabric	¼ yard	½ yard	1 yard
White fabric	1⅛ yards	2⅞ yards	6 yards
Backing fabric	2½ yards	3⅞ yards	8¾ yards
Binding fabric	⅓ yard	½ yard	¾ yard
Batting	44″ × 44″	68″ × 80″	104″ × 104″

Main Quilt Block
Fabric: Bella Solids by Moda Fabrics

Alternate Colorway

Cutting

	Cut	Baby 9 blocks	Throw 30 blocks	Coverlet 64 blocks
From gray fabric	2½″ × 2½″ squares	9	30	64
	2½″ × 4½″ strips	9	30	64
	2½″ × 6½″ strips	9	30	64
	2½″ × 8½″ strips	9	30	64
	2½″ × 10½″ strips	9	30	64
From red fabric	2½″ × 2½″ squares	27	90	192
From white fabric	2½″ × 2½″ squares	9	30	64
	2½″ × 4½″ strips	9	30	64
	2½″ × 6½″ strips	9	30	64
	2½″ × 8½″ strips	9	30	64
	2½″ × 10½″ strips	18	60	128

Sewing the Block

Seam allowances are ¼″ unless otherwise indicated. Press block after each step.

1. Use a red 2½″ square to make a snowball corner (page 6) at an end of a 10½″ strip. Note the angle placement (Figure A).

2. Sew a red 2½″ square to the snowball end of the unit from Step 1 (Figure B). Set aside.

Metropolis block

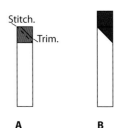

Stitch.

Trim.

A   B

3. Use a red 2½″ square to make a snowball corner at an end of another 10½″ strip. Make the angle in the opposite direction of the unit in Step 1 (Figure C). Set aside.

Stitch.

Trim.

C   D

4. Sew a white 2½″ square to the left side of a gray 2½″ square (Figure D).

5. Sew a white 2½″ × 4½″ strip to the top of the unit from Step 4 (Figure E).

E   F

6. Sew a gray 2½″ × 4½″ strip to the left side of the unit and a gray 2½″ × 6½″ strip to the top (Figure F).

7. Sew a white 2½″ × 6½″ strip to the left side of the unit and a white 2½″ × 8½″ strip to the top (Figure G).

8. Sew a gray 2½″ × 8½″ strip to the left side of the unit and a gray 2½″ × 10½″ strip to the top of the unit from Step 7 (Figure H).

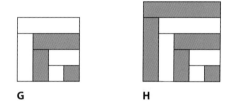

G   H

9. Sew the unit from Step 3 to the top of the unit from Step 8 (Figure I).

10. Referring to the Metropolis block diagram, sew the unit from Step 2 to the left side of the unit from Step 9 to complete the block.

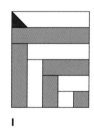

11. Repeat these steps to make the number of blocks needed (*baby size:* 9 blocks; *throw:* 30 blocks; *coverlet:* 64 blocks).

I

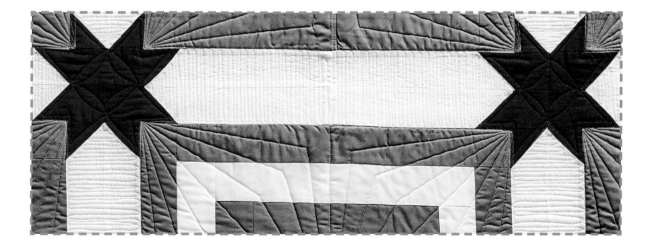

Putting It All Together

Refer to the *Metropolis* quilt assembly diagram to find the size quilt you are making. Note the block placement and alternate every other block within each row. Place the odd rows with the red squares at the top and the even rows with the red squares at the bottom.

- For the baby size, sew 3 rows of 3 blocks.

- For the throw, sew 6 rows of 5 blocks.

- For the coverlet, sew 8 rows of 8 blocks.

Press the seams in alternating directions from row to row.

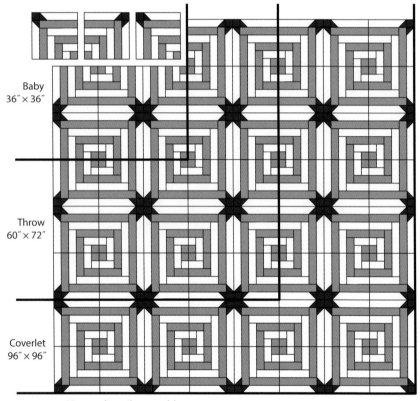

Baby
36″ × 36″

Throw
60″ × 72″

Coverlet
96″ × 96″

Metropolis quilt assembly

Finishing

Refer to Finishing the Quilt (page 9) to layer, quilt, and bind the quilt.

Metropolis coverlet, 96˝ × 96˝

Nonchalant

FINISHED SIZE: 99″ × 99″ • **BLOCK SIZE:** 123/8″ × 123/8″

Designed, pieced, and quilted by Natalia Bonner and Kathleen Whiting

Nonchalant is an easy one-block quilt made in just two colors plus white. Make blocks in two color-ways that are almost negative images of each other to create a lively addition to any room. Choose two of your favorite fabrics and a nice neutral background color, and you'll be ready!

Materials

Yardages are based on fabric that is at least 40″ wide.

	Baby 37⅛″ × 37⅛″	Throw 61⅞″ × 74¼″	Coverlet 99″ × 99″
☐ Gray fabric	⅝ yard	1⅔ yards	3½ yards
☐ Mustard fabric	⅓ yard	⅝ yard	1⅜ yards
☐ White fabric	1⅛ yard	3½ yards	7⅛ yards
Backing fabric	2½ yards	4⅔ yards	9 yards
Binding fabric	⅓ yard	⅝ yard	¾ yard
Batting	45″ × 45″	70″ × 82″	107″ × 107″

Main Quilt Block
Fabric: Bella Solids by Moda Fabrics

Alternate Colorway

Cutting

	Cut	Baby 9 blocks	Throw 30 blocks	Coverlet 64 blocks
From gray fabric	1⅞″ × 3¼″ strips	16	60	128
	1⅞″ × 4⅝″ strips	36	120	256
	1⅞″ × 6″ strips	20	60	128
From mustard fabric	1⅞″ × 1⅞″ squares	36	120	256
	1⅞″ × 3¼″ strips	20	60	128
From white fabric	1⅞″ × 1⅞″ squares	36	120	256
	1⅞″ × 3¼″ strips	36	120	256
	1⅞″ × 4⅝″ strips	36	120	256
	1⅞″ × 6″ strips	34	120	256
	1⅞″ × 12⅞″ strips	9	30	64

Sewing the Blocks

Seam allowances are ¼″ unless otherwise indicated. Press blocks after each step.

Nonchalant Block 1

1. Sew a mustard 1⅞″ square to the right side of a white 1⅞″ square (Figure A).

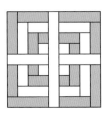
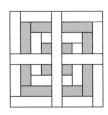

Nonchalant block 1   Nonchalant block 2

TIP

Step 1 is the same two-square unit for both Nonchalant block 1 and Nonchalant block 2. If you wish, you can strip piece (page 8) to complete all the units at one time.

2. Sew a mustard 1⅞″ × 3¼″ strip to the top of the unit from Step 1 (Figure B).

3. Sew a white 1⅞″ × 3¼″ strip to the right side of the unit and a white 1⅞″ × 4⅝″ strip to the top (Figure C).

A   B   C

4. Sew a gray 1⅞″ × 4⅝″ strip to the right side of the unit and a gray 1⅞″ × 6″ strip to the top (Figure D).

5. Repeat Steps 1–4 to make 3 more units.

6. Sew a white 1⅞″ × 6″ strip between 2 units from Step 5. Make 2 (Figure E).

7. Referring to the Nonchalant block 1 diagram, sew a white 1⅞″ × 12⅞″ strip between the 2 units from Step 6 to complete the block.

8. Repeat these steps to make the number of blocks needed (*baby size:* 5 blocks; *throw:* 15 blocks; *coverlet:* 32 blocks).

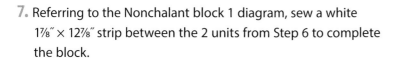

D   E

Nonchalant Block 2

1. Sew a white 1⅞″ square to the right side of a mustard 1⅞″ square (Figure F).

2. Sew a white 1⅞″ × 3¼″ strip to the top of the unit from Step 1 (Figure G).

3. Sew a gray 1⅞″ × 3¼″ strip to the right side of the unit and a gray 1⅞″ × 4⅝″ strip to the top (Figure H).

4. Sew a white 1⅞″ × 4⅝″ strip to the right side of the unit and a white 1⅞″ × 6″ strip to the top of the unit (Figure I).

5. Repeat Steps 1–4 to make 3 more units.

6. Sew a white 1⅞″ × 6″ strip between 2 units from Step 5. Make 2 (Figure J).

7. Referring to the Nonchalant block 2 diagram, sew a white 1⅞″ × 12⅞″ strip between the 2 units from Step 6 to complete the block.

8. Repeat these steps to make the number of blocks needed (*baby size:* 4 blocks; *throw:* 15 blocks; *coverlet:* 32 blocks).

F   G

H   I

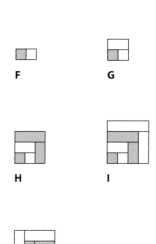

J

Putting It All Together

Refer to the *Nonchalant* quilt assembly diagram to find the size quilt you are making. Note the block placement. Alternate between block 1 and block 2 in each row. Start odd rows with block 1 and even rows with block 2.

- For the baby quilt, use 5 of block 1 and 4 of block 2. Sew 3 rows of 3 blocks.

- For the throw, use 15 each of block 1 and block 2. Sew 6 rows of 5 blocks.

- For the coverlet, use 32 each of block 1 and block 2. Sew 8 rows of 8 blocks.

Press the seams in alternating directions from row to row.

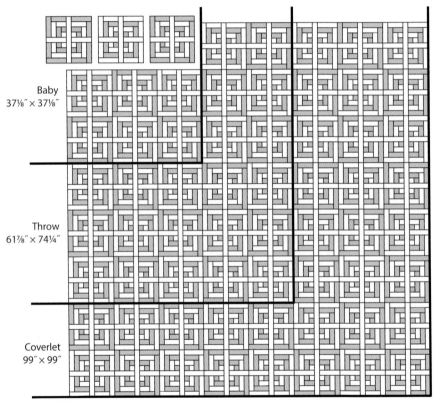

Baby
37⅛" × 37⅛"

Throw
61⅞" × 74¼"

Coverlet
99" × 99"

Nonchalant quilt assembly

Finishing

Refer to Finishing the Quilt (page 9) to layer, quilt, and bind the quilt.

Nonchalant coverlet, 99″ × 99″

Outstretched

FINISHED SIZE: 96″ × 96″ • **BLOCK SIZE:** 12″ × 12″

Designed, pieced, and quilted by Natalia Bonner and Kathleen Whiting

There's a bit of an optical illusion here. These elongated, framed rectangles look like we stretched a traditional Log Cabin quilt block, but they're really made from two identical 12"-square blocks. We limited the color palette to two colors to really emphasize the graphic nature of the blocks, but this could be very interesting in a wider color range!

Materials

Yardages are based on fabric that is at least 40" wide.

	Baby 36" × 36"	Throw 60" × 72"	Coverlet 96" × 96"
■ Spruce fabric	1⅛ yards	3⅛ yards	6½ yards
□ Ivory fabric	1 yard	2½ yards	5 yards
Backing fabric	2½ yards	3⅞ yards	8¾ yards
Binding fabric	⅓ yard	½ yard	¾ yard
Batting	44" × 44"	68" × 80"	104" × 104"

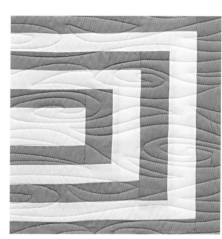

Main Quilt Block
Fabric: Art Gallery Fabrics

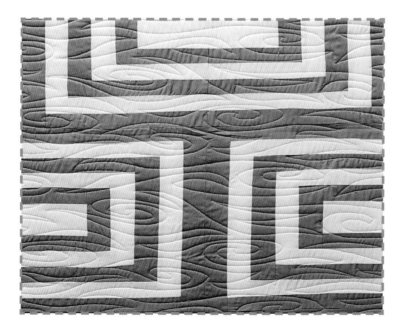

Alternate Colorway

Cutting

	Cut	Baby 9 blocks	Throw 30 blocks	Coverlet 64 blocks
From spruce fabric	1½″ × 5″ strips	18	60	128
	2″ × 4½″ strips	9	30	64
	1½″ × 8″ strips	18	60	128
	2″ × 8½″ strips	9	30	64
	1½″ × 11″ strips	18	60	128
	2″ × 12½″ strips	9	30	64
From ivory fabric	2½″ × 5″ strips	9	30	64
	1½″ × 6½″ strips	18	60	128
	2″ × 6½″ strips	9	30	64
	1½″ × 9½″ strips	18	60	128
	2″ × 10½″ strips	9	30	64

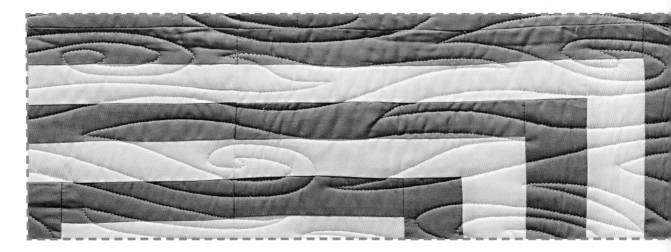

Sewing the Block

Seam allowances are ¼″ unless otherwise indicated. Press block after each step.

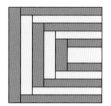

Outstretched block

1. Sew 2 spruce 1½″ × 5″ strips to the top and bottom of an ivory 2½″ × 5″ strip (Figure A).

2. Sew a spruce 2″ × 4½″ strip to the left side of the unit from Step 1 (Figure B).

3. Sew an ivory 1½″ × 6½″ strip to the top and bottom of the unit and an ivory 2″ × 6½″ strip to the left side (Figure C).

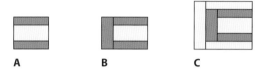

A   B   C

4. Sew a spruce 1½″ × 8″ strip to the top and bottom of the unit and a spruce 2″ × 8½″ strip to the left side (Figure D).

5. Sew an ivory 1½″ × 9½″ strip to the top and bottom of the unit and an ivory 2″ × 10½″ strip to the left side (Figure E).

6. Referring to the Outstretched block diagram, sew a spruce 1½″ × 11″ strip to the top and bottom of the unit and a spruce 2″ × 12½″ strip to the left side to complete the block.

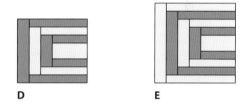

D   E

7. Repeat these steps to make the number of blocks needed (*baby size:* 9 blocks; *throw:* 30 blocks; *coverlet:* 64 blocks).

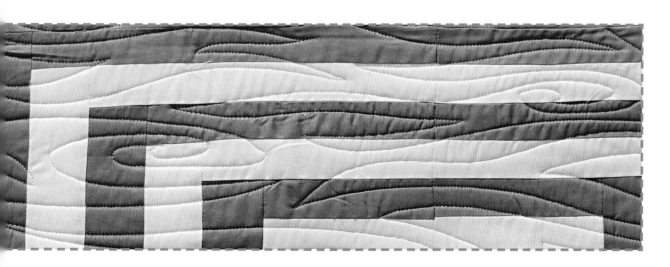

Putting It All Together

Refer to the *Outstretched* quilt assembly diagram to find the size quilt you are making. Note the block placement and alternate the direction of every other block within the rows.

- For the baby size, sew 3 rows of 3 blocks.

- For the throw, sew 6 rows of 5 blocks.

- For the coverlet, sew 8 rows of 8 blocks.

Press the seams in alternating directions from row to row.

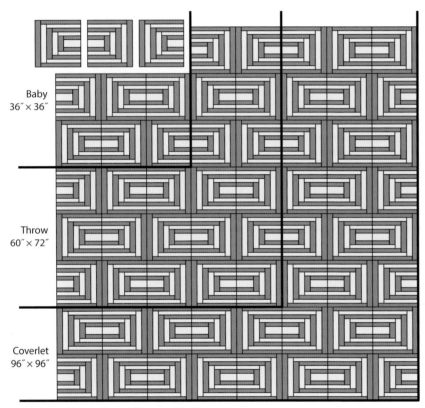

Outstretched quilt assembly diagram

Finishing

Refer to Finishing the Quilt (page 9) to layer, quilt, and bind the quilt.

Outstretched coverlet, 96˝ × 96˝

Peaches and Cream

FINISHED SIZE: 96″ × 96″ • **BLOCK SIZE:** 12″ × 12″

Designed and quilted by Natalia Bonner and Kathleen Whiting; pieced by Ilene Peterson and Emmy Jasperson

A large repeating block appears when you set four blocks together in this graphic quilt. The warm coral and gold fabrics draw the eye, while the soft blues add a restful frame in the background. White strips create a strong allover grid and a modern vibe.

Materials

Yardages are based on fabric that is at least 40″ wide.

	Baby 36″ × 36″	Throw 60″ × 72″	Coverlet 96″ × 96″
Sun fabric	¼ yard	½ yard	¾ yard
Coral fabric	½ yard	1 yard	1⅞ yards
White fabric	⅔ yard	1⅝ yards	3⅓ yards
Dark blue fabric	½ yard	1 yard	2 yards
Light blue fabric	⅔ yard	1⅜ yards	2⅞ yards
Backing fabric	2½ yards	3⅞ yards	8¾ yards
Binding fabric	⅓ yard	½ yard	¾ yard
Batting	44″ × 44″	68″ × 80″	104″ × 104″

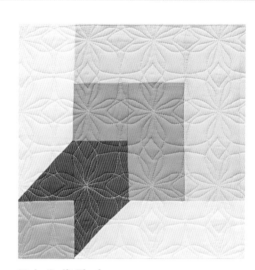

Main Quilt Block
Fabric: Birch Fabrics

Alternate Colorway

Cutting

	Cut	Baby 9 blocks	Throw 30 blocks	Coverlet 64 blocks
From sun fabric	3½″ × 3½″ squares	9	30	64
From coral fabric	3½″ × 3½″ squares	27	90	192
From white fabric	3½″ × 9½″ strips	18	60	128
From dark blue fabric	3½″ × 3½″ squares	9	30	64
	3½″ × 6½″ strips	9	30	64
From light blue fabric	3½″ × 6½″ strips	9	30	64
	3½″ × 9½″ strips	9	30	64

Sewing the Block

Seam allowances are ¼″ unless otherwise indicated. Press block after each step.

1. Use a coral 3½″ square to make a snowball corner (page 6) on a short end of a white 3½″ × 9½″ strip. Note placement of the angle. (Figure A)

2. Sew a sun 3½″ square to the snowball end of the unit from Step 1 (Figure B). Set aside.

3. Use a coral 3½″ square to make a snowball corner on the short end of another 9½″ strip. Make the angle in the opposite direction of the unit in Step 1 (Figure C). Set aside.

4. Sew a dark blue 3½″ square to the left side of a coral 3½″ square (Figure D).

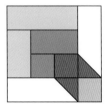

Peaches and Cream block

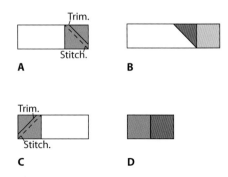

5. Sew a dark blue 3½″ × 6½″ strip to the top of the unit from Step 4 (Figure E).

6. Sew a light blue 3½″ × 6½″ strip to the left side of the unit from Step 4 and a light blue 3½″ × 9½″ strip to the top (Figure F).

E   F

7. Sew the unit from Step 3 to the right side of the unit from Step 6 (Figure G).

8. Referring to the Peaches and Cream block diagram, sew the unit from Step 2 to the bottom of the unit to complete the block.

9. Repeat these steps to make the number of blocks needed (*baby size:* 9 blocks; *throw:* 30 blocks; *coverlet:* 64 blocks).

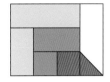

G

Putting It All Together

Refer to the *Peaches and Cream* quilt assembly diagram to find the size quilt you are making.

- For the baby size, sew 3 rows of 3 blocks.

- For the throw, sew 6 rows of 5 blocks.

- For the coverlet, sew 8 rows of 8 blocks.

Press the seams in alternating directions from row to row.

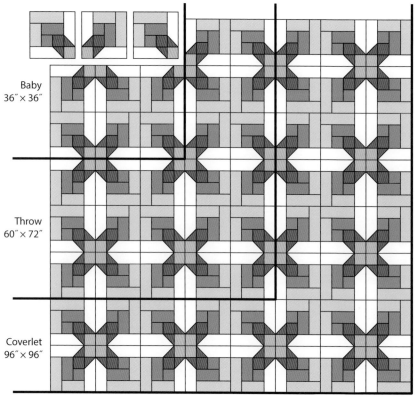

Baby
36″ × 36″

Throw
60″ × 72″

Coverlet
96″ × 96″

Peaches and Cream quilt assembly

Finishing

Refer to Finishing the Quilt (page 9) to layer, quilt, and bind the quilt.

Peaches and Cream coverlet, 96″ × 96″

Pinwheel Cabins

FINISHED SIZE: 96″ × 96″ • **BLOCK SIZE:** 12″ × 12″

Designed, pieced, and quilted by Natalia Bonner and Kathleen Whiting

Pinwheel Cabins is a fun, simple, modern version of a traditional Log Cabin quilt, with just one round of logs around the center square. To add dimension, we added angled corners to the frames. These are so easy to make with the snowball method (page 6).

We limited our color choices to one print and two solid fabrics. But the large squares give you the chance to show off a variety of prints from your stash, or finally use that stack of 10″ squares that you couldn't resist!

Materials
Yardages are based on fabric that is at least 40″ wide.

	Baby 36″ × 36″	Throw 60″ × 72″	Coverlet 96″ × 96″
◼ Tan fabric	½ yard	1½ yards	3⅛ yards
☐ Ivory fabric	⅝ yard	1½ yards	3 yards
☐ Print fabric	1 yard	2⅛ yards	4⅛ yards
Backing fabric	2½ yards	3⅞ yards	8¾ yards
Binding fabric	⅓ yard	½ yard	¾ yard
Batting	44″ × 44″	68″ × 80″	104″ × 104″

TIP

This quilt would be a great way to use up your stash or a layer cake.

Main Quilt Block
Fabric: Chromatics and Pure Elements by Art Gallery Fabrics

Alternate Colorway

Cutting

	Cut:	Baby 9 blocks	Throw 30 blocks	Coverlet 64 blocks
From tan fabric	2½″ × 12½″ strips	18	60	128
From ivory fabric	2½″ × 2½″ squares	18	60	128
	2½″ × 8½″ strips	18	60	128
From print fabric	8½″ × 8½″ squares	9	30	64

Sewing the Block

Seam allowances are ¼″ unless otherwise indicated. Press block after each step.

1. Use an ivory 2½″ square to make a snowball corner (page 6) on a short end of a tan 2½″ × 12½″ strip. Note placement of the angle. Make 2 and set aside (Figure A).

2. Sew 2 ivory 2½″ × 8½″ strips to opposite sides of the print 8½″ square (Figure B).

3. Referring to the Pinwheel Cabins block diagram, sew the units from Step 1 to the top and bottom of the unit from Step 2.

4. Repeat these steps to make the number of blocks needed (*baby size:* 9 blocks; *throw:* 30 blocks; *coverlet:* 64 blocks).

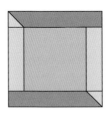

Pinwheel Cabins block

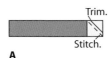

Trim.

Stitch.

A

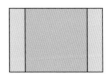

B

Putting It All Together

Refer to the *Pinwheel Cabins* quilt assembly diagram to find the size quilt you are making. Note the block placement and alternate the direction of every other block within the rows.

- For the baby size, sew 3 rows of 3 blocks.
- For the throw, sew 6 rows of 5 blocks.
- For the coverlet, sew 8 rows of 8 blocks.

Press the seams in alternating directions from row to row.

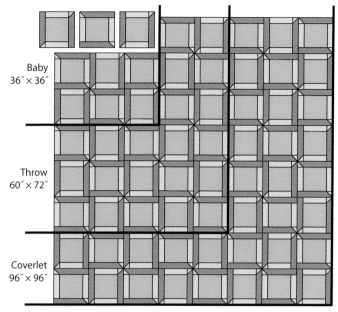

Pinwheel Cabins quilt assembly

Finishing

Refer to Finishing the Quilt (page 9) to layer, quilt, and bind the quilt.

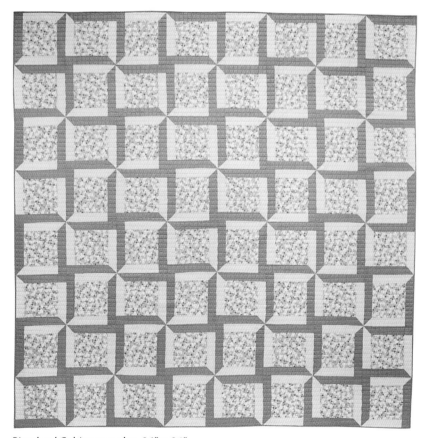

Pinwheel Cabins coverlet, 96″ × 96″

Pushover

FINISHED SIZE: 96″ × 96″ • **BLOCK SIZE:** 12″ × 12″

Designed, pieced, and quilted by Natalia Bonner and Kathleen Whiting

Pushover is a sweet mix of soft pink, yellow, and white. The negative white space in this quilt lends itself to so many ideas. If you make the outer logs of the block in a color instead of white, or half the blocks in one color and the other half in another, it would give a completely different look to the quilt. You could make it entirely scrappy, or pull some masculine fabrics for your favorite guy.

Materials

Yardages are based on fabric that is at least 40" wide.

	Baby 36" × 36"	Throw 60" × 72"	Coverlet 96" × 96"
Pink fabric	½ yard	1 yard	2 yards
Yellow fabric	¼ yard	½ yard	¾ yard
White fabric	1⅛ yards	3⅛ yards	6⅔ yards
Backing fabric	2½ yards	3⅞ yards	8¾ yards
Binding fabric	⅓ yard	½ yard	¾ yard
Batting	44" × 44"	68" × 80"	104" × 104"

Main Quilt Block
Fabric: Art Gallery Fabrics

Cutting

	Cut	Baby 9 blocks	Throw 30 blocks	Coverlet 64 blocks
From white fabric	3½" × 6½" strips	9	30	64
	3½" × 9½" strips	18	60	128
	3½" × 12½" strips	9	30	64
From yellow fabric	3½" × 3½" squares	9	30	64
From pink fabric	3½" × 3½" squares	9	30	64
	3½" × 6½" strips	9	30	64

Alternate Colorway

Sewing the Block

Seam allowances are ¼″ unless otherwise indicated. Press after each step.

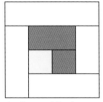

Pushover block

1. Sew a pink 3½″ square to the right side of a yellow 3½″ square (Figure A).

2. Sew a pink 3½″ × 6½″ strip to top of the unit from Step 1 (Figure B).

3. Sew a white 3½″ × 6½″ strip to the right side of the unit and a white 3½″ × 9½″ strip to the bottom (Figure C).

4. Referring to the Pushover quilt block diagram, sew a white 3½″ × 9½″ strip to the left side of the unit and a white 3½″ × 12½″ strip to the top to complete the block.

5. Repeat these steps to make the number of blocks needed (*baby size:* 9 blocks; *throw:* 30 blocks; *coverlet:* 64 blocks).

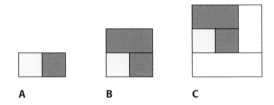

A   **B**   **C**

Putting It All Together

Refer to the *Pushover* quilt assembly diagram to find the size quilt you are making. Note the block placement and alternate the direction of every other block within the rows.

- For the baby size, sew 3 rows of 3 blocks.

- For the throw, sew 6 rows of 5 blocks.

- For the coverlet, sew 8 rows of 8 blocks.

Press the seams in alternating directions from row to row.

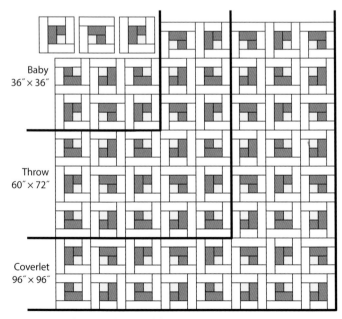

Baby
36″ × 36″

Throw
60″ × 72″

Coverlet
96″ × 96″

Pushover quilt assembly

Finishing

Refer to Finishing the Quilt (page 9) to layer, quilt, and bind the quilt.

Pushover coverlet, 96˝ × 96˝

Radiance

FINISHED SIZE: 96″ × 96″ • BLOCK SIZE: 12″ × 12″

Designed, pieced, and quilted by Natalia Bonner and Kathleen Whiting

This quilt looks difficult to make, but it's really an easy combination of a quarter Log Cabin block with stitch-and-flip snowball corners (page 6). You will have some small triangles left over, but set those aside for use in another quilt.

Materials

Yardages are based on fabric that is at least 40″ wide.

	Baby 36″ × 36″	Throw 60″ × 72″	Coverlet 96″ × 96″
Yellow fabric	1⅛ yards	2⅞ yards	5⅞ yards
Turquoise fabric	1⅛ yards	2½ yards	4⅞ yards
White fabric	⅞ yard	2⅛ yards	4¼ yards
Backing fabric	2½ yards	3⅞ yards	8¾ yards
Binding fabric	⅓ yard	½ yard	¾ yard
Batting	44″ × 44″	68″ × 80″	104″ × 104″

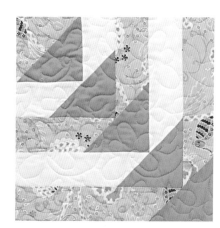

Main Quilt Block
Fabric: FreeSpirit Fabrics

--- **TIP** ---

Use a high-contrast fabric for the triangles to really make the pattern pop.

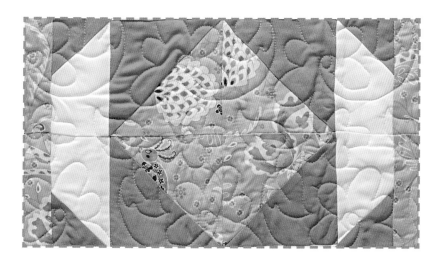

Alternate Colorway

Cutting

	Cut	Baby 9 blocks	Throw 30 blocks	Coverlet 64 blocks
From yellow fabric	4⅞″ × 4⅞″ squares	5	15	32
	2½″ × 6½″ strips	9	30	64
	2½″ × 8½″ strips	9	30	64
	2½″ × 10½″ strips	9	30	64
	2½″ × 12½″ strips	9	30	64
From turquoise fabric	4⅞″ × 4⅞″ squares	5	15	32
	4½″ × 4½″ squares	36	120	256
From white fabric	2½″ × 4½″ strips	9	30	64
	2½″ × 6½″ strips	9	30	64
	2½″ × 8½″ strips	9	30	64
	2½″ × 10½″ strips	9	30	64

Sewing the Block

Seam allowances are ¼″ unless otherwise indicated. Press block after each step.

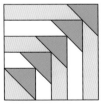

Radiance block

1. Using a yellow 4⅞″ square and a turquoise 4⅞″ square, make 2 half-square triangles using the No-Waste Method (page 7). Set a unit aside for another block (Figure A).

2. Sew a white 2½″ × 4½″ strip to the right side of the unit from Step 1 and a white 2½″ × 6½″ strip to the top (Figure B).

3. Use a turquoise 4½″ square to make a snowball corner (page 6) on the top right corner of the unit from Step 2 (Figure C).

A

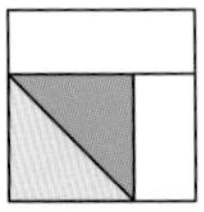

B

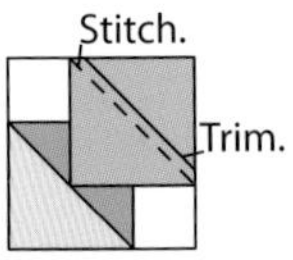

Stitch.

Trim.

C

4. Sew a yellow 2½″ × 6½″ strip to the top of the unit and a yellow 2½″ × 8½″ strip to the right side (Figure D).

5. Use a turquoise 4½″ square to make a snowball corner on the top right corner of the unit from Step 4 (Figure E).

D   **E**

6. Sew a white 2½″ × 8½″ strip to the top of the unit and a white 2½″ × 10½″ strip to the right side (Figure F).

7. Use a turquoise 4½″ square to make a snowball corner on the top right corner of the unit from Step 6 (Figure G).

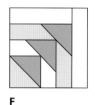

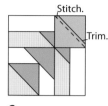

8. Sew a yellow 2½″ × 10½″ strip to the top of the unit and a yellow 2½″ × 12½″ strip to the right side (Figure H).

F   **G**

9. Referring to the Radiance block diagram, use a turquoise 4½″ square to make a snowball corner on the top right corner of the unit to complete the block.

10. Repeat these steps to make the number of blocks needed (*baby size:* 9 blocks; *throw:* 30 blocks; *coverlet:* 64 blocks).

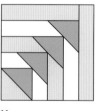

H

Putting It All Together

Refer to the *Radiance* quilt assembly diagram to find the size quilt you are making. Note the block placement and alternate the direction of every other block within each row.

- For the baby size, sew 3 rows of 3 blocks.

- For the throw, sew 6 rows of 5 blocks.

- For the coverlet, sew 8 rows of 8 blocks.

Press the seams in alternating directions from row to row.

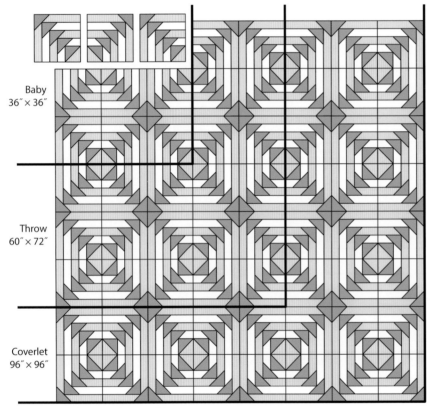

Baby
36˝ × 36˝

Throw
60˝ × 72˝

Coverlet
96˝ × 96˝

Radiance quilt assembly

Finishing

Refer to Finishing the Quilt (page 9) to layer, quilt, and bind the quilt.

Radiance coverlet, 96″ × 96″

Stacked Up

FINISHED SIZE: 102″ × 102″ • **BLOCK SIZE:** 12″ × 12″

Designed, pieced, and quilted by Natalia Bonner and Kathleen Whiting

Stacked Up *is a cool variation of a Log Cabin quilt block. Fabric placement is key in this quilt, giving the quilt the look of blocks stacked on each other.*

Materials
Yardages are based on fabric that is at least 40˝ wide.

	Baby 34˝ × 34˝	Throw 68˝ × 68˝	Coverlet 102˝ × 102˝
Orange fabric	¾ yard	1⅛ yards	1½ yards
Green fabric		1⅛ yards	1½ yards
Pink fabric			1½ yards
Sand fabric	½ yard	1 yard	1⅞ yards
White fabric	1½ yards	3¼ yards	6⅞ yards
Backing fabric	2½ yards	4¼ yards	9⅜ yards
Binding fabric	⅓ yard	⅝ yard	¾ yard
Batting	42˝ × 42˝	76˝ × 76˝	110˝ × 110˝

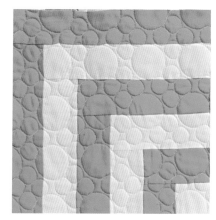

Main Quilt Block
Fabric: Bella Solids by Moda Fabrics

Alternate Colorway

TIP

This quilt would be a great quilt to use up jelly roll strips.

Cutting

	Cut	Baby 7 blocks	Throw 26 blocks	Coverlet 57 blocks
From orange fabric	2½″ × 2½″ squares	5	9	13
	2½″ × 4½″ strips	5	9	13
	2½″ × 6½″ strips	5	9	13
	2½″ × 8½″ strips	5	9	13
	2½″ × 10½″ strips	5	9	13
	2½″ × 12½″ strips	5	9	13
From green fabric	2½″ × 2½″ squares		9	13
	2½″ × 4½″ strips		9	13
	2½″ × 6½″ strips		9	13
	2½″ × 8½″ strips		9	13
	2½″ × 10½″ strips		9	13
	2½″ × 12½″ strips		9	13
From pink fabric	2½″ × 2½″ squares			13
	2½″ × 4½″ strips			13
	2½″ × 6½″ strips			13
	2½″ × 8½″ strips			13
	2½″ × 10½″ strips			13
	2½″ × 12½″ strips			13
From sand fabric	2½″ × 2½″ squares	2	8	18
	2½″ × 4½″ strips	2	8	18
	2½″ × 6½″ strips	2	8	18
	2½″ × 8½″ strips	2	8	18
	2½″ × 10½″ strips	2	8	18
	2½″ × 12½″ strips	2	8	18
From white fabric	2½″ × 2½″ squares	7	26	57
	2½″ × 4½″ strips	7	26	57
	2½″ × 6½″ strips	7	26	57
	2½″ × 8½″ strips	7	26	57
	2½″ × 10½″ strips	7	26	57
	12½″ × 12½″ squares		3	10
	18¼″ × 18¼″ for setting triangles	1	2	4
	93/8″ × 93/8″ for corner triangles	2	2	2

Sewing the Block

Seam allowances are ¼″ unless otherwise indicated. Press after each step.

1. Sew a color 2½″ square to the right side of a white 2½″ square (Figure A).

2. Sew a color 2½″ × 4½″ strip to the top of the unit from Step 1 (Figure B).

3. Sew a white 2½″ × 4½″ strip to the right side of the unit and a white 2½″ × 6½″ strip to the top (Figure C).

4. Sew a color 2½″ × 6½″ strip to the right side of the unit and a color 2½″ × 8½″ strip to the top (Figure D).

5. Sew a white 2½″ × 8½″ strip to the right side of the unit and a white 2½″ × 10½″ strip to the top (Figure E).

6. Referring to the Stacked Up block diagram, sew a color 2½″ × 10½″ strip to the right side of the unit and a color 2½″ × 12½″ strip to the top to complete the block.

7. Repeat these steps to make the number of blocks needed (*baby size:* 5 orange and 2 sand; *throw:* 9 each of green and orange, 8 sand; *coverlet:* 13 each of green, orange, and pink, 18 sand).

Pieced Setting Triangles

To make setting triangles for the quilt's outer edges, cut blocks in half diagonally ¼″ from the centerline as shown. The small white square will be at the center tip of setting triangle A; the red outer edge of the block will be at the center tip of setting triangle B.

For the baby quilt, you will need 1 each of setting triangles A and B in orange (2 total).

For the throw, you will need 1 each of setting triangles A and B in orange and green (4 total).

For the coverlet, you will need 1 each of setting triangles A and B in orange, green, and pink (6 total).

TIP

Fabric placement is key in this quilt.

Refer to layout for proper placement.

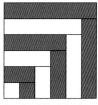

Stacked Up block

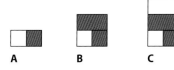

A   B   C

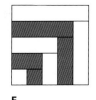

D   E

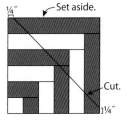

¼″   Set aside. — Cut. ¼″

Setting triangle A

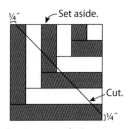

¼″   Set aside. — Cut. ¼″

Setting triangle B

Putting It All Together

Refer to the *Stacked Up* quilt assembly diagram for the size quilt you are making. Arrange the blocks and setting triangles in diagonal rows. Note the block placement.

Stacked Up baby quilt assembly, finished 34˝ × 34˝

- For the baby size, use 5 blocks, 4 corner triangles, 2 white setting triangles, and 2 pieced setting triangles.

- For the throw, use 22 blocks, 3 white squares, 4 corner triangles, 8 white setting triangles, and 4 pieced setting triangles.

- For the coverlet, use 51 blocks, 10 white squares, 4 corner triangles, 14 white setting triangles, and 6 pieced setting triangles.

Press the seams in alternating directions from row to row.

Stacked Up throw quilt assembly, finished 68˝ × 68˝

Stacked Up coverlet quilt assembly, finished 102˝ × 102˝

Finishing

Refer to Finishing the Quilt (page 9) to layer, quilt, and bind the quilt.

Stacked Up coverlet, 102″ × 102″

Typhoon

FINISHED SIZE: 96″ × 96″ • **BLOCK SIZE:** 12″ × 12″

Designed, pieced, and quilted by Natalia Bonner and Kathleen Whiting

Typhoon is a cool twist, literally, on a Log Cabin–style quilt block. Pick out eight of your favorite fabrics and match them with a white and a gray fabric. This quilt is a fantastic quilt to show off your larger-scale prints.

Materials

Yardages are based on fabric that is at least 40″ wide.

	Baby 36″ × 36″	Throw 60″ × 72″	Coverlet 96″ × 96″
Purple 1 fabric	⅓ yard	⅓ yard	⅓ yard
Purple 2 fabric	½ yard	⅔ yard	⅔ yard
Purple 3 fabric	⅓ yard	⅞ yard	1 yard
Purple 4 fabric		⅔ yard	1⅛ yards
Purple 5 fabric		⅓ yard	1 yard
Purple 6 fabric			⅞ yard
Purple 7 fabric			½ yard
Purple 8 fabric			⅓ yard
White fabric	⅔ yard	1⅝ yards	3⅛ yards
Gray fabric	1 yard	2⅓ yards	4⅔ yards
Backing fabric	2½ yards	3⅞ yards	8¾ yards
Binding fabric	⅓ yard	½ yard	¾ yard
Batting	44″ × 44″	68″ × 80″	104″ × 104″

TIP

This quilt would be a great quilt to use up your stash or a few fat quarters.

Main Quilt Block
Fabric: Art Gallery Fabrics

Alternate Colorway

Cutting

	Cut	Baby 9 blocks	Throw 30 blocks	Coverlet 64 blocks
From purple 1 fabric	5½″ × 7½″ strips	3	3	3
	5½″ × 5½″ squares	3	3	3
From purple 2 fabric	5½″ × 7½″ strips	5	7	7
	5½″ × 5½″ squares	5	7	7
From purple 3 fabric	5½″ × 7½″ strips	1	10	11
	5½″ × 5½″ squares	1	10	11
From purple 4 fabric	5½″ × 7½″ strips		7	15
	5½″ × 5½″ squares		7	15
From purple 5 fabric	5½″ × 7½″ strips		3	13
	5½″ × 5½″ squares		3	13
From purple 6 fabric	5½″ × 7½″ strips			9
	5½″ × 5½″ squares			9
From purple 7 fabric	5½″ × 7½″ strips			5
	5½″ × 5½″ squares			5
From purple 8 fabric	5½″ × 7½″ strips			1
	5½″ × 5½″ squares			1
From white fabric	5½″ × 7½″ strips	9	30	64
	2½″ × 7½″ strips	9	30	64
From gray fabric	5½″ × 12½″ strips	9	30	64
	4½″ × 4½″ squares	9	30	64

Sewing the Block

Seam allowances are ¼″ unless otherwise indicated. Press after each step.

1. Use a gray 4½″ square to make a snowball corner (page 6) on the top left corner of a 5½″ × 7½″ white strip (Figure A).

2. Use a purple 5½″ square to make a snowball corner on the bottom right corner of the unit from Step 1. Set aside (Figure B).

3. Sew a matching purple 5½″ × 7½″ strip to the bottom of a white 2½″ × 7½″ strip (Figure C).

4. Sew the unit from Step 2 to the left side of the unit from Step 3 (Figure D).

5. Referring to the Typhoon block diagram, sew a gray 5½″ × 12½″ strip to the top of the unit from Step 4 to complete the block.

6. Repeat these steps to make the number of blocks needed (*baby size:* 9 blocks; *throw:* 30 blocks; *coverlet:* 64 blocks).

Typhoon block

TIP

Fabric placement is key in this quilt. Refer to illustrations to get it correct.

Trim.
Stitch.

A

B

C

D

Putting It All Together

Refer to the *Typhoon* quilt assembly diagram to find the size quilt you are making. Note the block placement for color and alternate the blocks within each row.

- For the baby size, sew 3 rows of 3 blocks.

- For the throw, sew 6 rows of 5 blocks.

- For the coverlet, sew 8 rows of 8 blocks.

Press the seams in alternating directions from row to row.

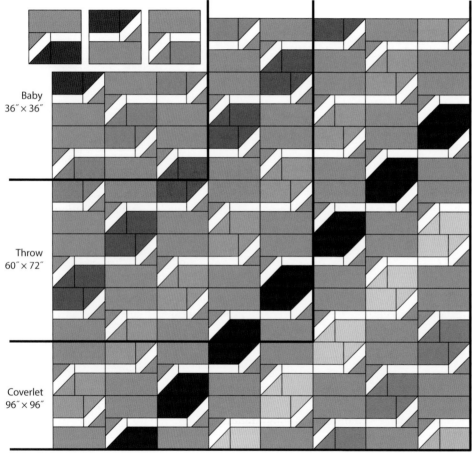

Typhoon quilt assembly

Finishing

Refer to Finishing the Quilt (page 9) to layer, quilt, and bind the quilt.

Typhoon coverlet, 96″ × 96″

Pillows

FINISHED SIZES: Simple throw pillow, 18″ × 18″;
pieced throw pillows, 16″ × 16″; pillow shams, 21″ × 32″

Designed, made, and quilted by Natalia Bonner and Kathleen Whiting

Throw pillows and shams are a great way to add a bit of color to any room. Give a custom look to either by machine quilting straight lines or circles onto plain fabric. Or use leftovers from the quilt projects to create a pieced pillow top.

Materials
Yardages are based on fabric that is at least 40˝ wide.

	Throw pillow	Pillow sham
Pillow front	¾ yard for simple throw pillow; none for pieced throw pillow	¾ yard
Pillow lining	¾ yard	¾ yard
Pillow back	⅜ yard	1¼ yards
Batting	¾ yard	¾ yard
Pillow form	20˝	20˝

TIP

These throw pillows and shams are a great way to use leftover fabric from your quilt tops or to bust your stash.

Cutting

	Simple throw pillow	*Dappled* or *Downtown Cabins* throw pillow	Pillow sham
Pillow front	1 square 24˝ × 24˝	No cutting necessary! Use 4 leftover half-blocks from the setting triangles for *Dappled* (page 24) or *Downtown Cabins* (page 40).	1 rectangle 21½˝ × 32½˝
Pillow lining	1 square 24˝ × 24˝	1 rectangle 20˝ × 20˝	1 rectangle 21½˝ × 32½˝
Pillow back	2 rectangles 11˝ × 19˝	2 rectangles 10½˝ × 16½˝	2 rectangles 20˝ × 21½˝

Making the Pieced Pillow Front

1. To make a pillow front from leftover triangles from the *Dappled* or *Downtown Cabins* quilts, sew the short sides of 2 triangles together (Figures A and B). Make 2.

2. Sew the triangle units together along the long diagonal edges to make a square (Figures C and D).

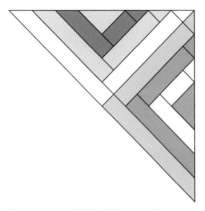

A. *Downtown Cabins* leftover triangles

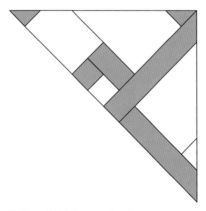

B. *Dappled* leftover triangles

C. *Downtown Cabins* pillow top

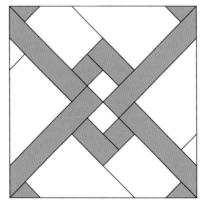

D. *Dapple* pillow top

Sewing the Pillow or Sham

Follow these simple construction steps to make any of the pillow or sham projects.
Seam allowances are ¼˝ unless otherwise indicated. Press after each step.

1. Stack in the following order from bottom up:

- Pillow lining, wrong side up

- Batting

- Pillow front fabric, right side up

Pin.

2. Quilt the pillow front as desired. For the throw pillows, we machine quilted straight lines ½˝ apart on the pillow front. For the pillow sham, we machine quilted circles all over the pillow front.

TIP

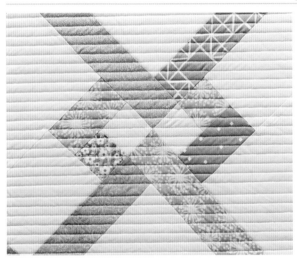

It helps to use a walking foot or even-feed foot for straight-line machine quilting. This foot moves fabric from the top while the feed dogs move it from the bottom, which helps feed the quilt layers through the machine smoothly.

For free-motion quilting such as the small circles for the pillow sham, use a hopping foot. With this foot, put the feed dogs down so you can freely move the fabric under the needle.

A walking foot helps feed the fabric smoothly during straight-line machine quilting.

Photo by Bernina USA

Use a hopping foot for free-motion quilting, like the circles on our pillow sham.

Photo by Bernina USA

3. Square up the tops:

- Simple throw pillow top: Trim to 19″ × 19″.

- Pillow sham: Trim to 21″ × 32″.

- Pieced pillow top: Sometimes the process of quilting causes a pieced block to go out of square. To square it up, place a piece of batting on the carpet. Lay the finished pillow top on top of the batting. Use a spray bottle to soak the top in water. Use a yardstick or carpenter's square to straighten the quilt top, and pin it in place with T-pins. Pin those T-pins right into the carpet to hold the quilt square. Leave the quilt overnight, until it has dried thoroughly. Sometimes I use a small fan to help the drying process.

4. Turn under ½″ along the long edge of each backing rectangle, and press. Fold again ½″ and press. Topstitch ⅛″ from the inner folded edge of each to create a hem.

5. Place the quilted pillow or sham front right side up. Place the pillow backing rectangles facedown on top of the quilted front, with the hemmed edges overlapping in the center and the raw edges of the backing aligned with the edges of the front. Pin. Stitch a ¼″ seam around the outside edge (Figure C).

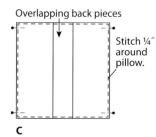

Overlapping back pieces

Stitch ¼″ around pillow.

6. Turn the pillow right side out. Topstitch 1″ from the edge around all 4 sides, creating a faux flange (refer to the photo of the blue completed pillow, page 125).

C

7. Insert the pillow form. We prefer to use a pillow form that is 2″ larger than the pillow size to give the pillow a fuller look.

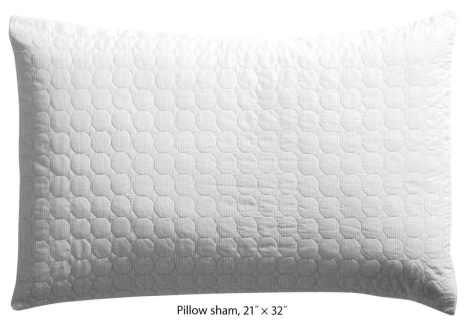

Pillow sham, 21″ × 32″

Dappled and *Downtown Cabins* pillows, 16″ × 16″

Simple throw pillow, 18″ × 18″

Resources

Moda Fabrics
unitednotions.com

Art Gallery Fabrics
artgalleryfabrics.com

Michael Miller Fabrics
michaelmillerfabrics.com

FreeSpirit
freespiritfabric.com

Quilters Dream Batting
quiltersdreambatting.com

Superior Threads
superiorthreads.com

About *the authors*

Photo by Whitnee North

Natalia Whiting Bonner has enjoyed piecing quilt tops for more than twenty years. She learned how to quilt on her conventional home machine. She felt good about it, but decided that if she really wanted to take her quilting to the next level, she needed to invest in a longarm machine. In 2007, when she was pregnant with her daughter, she got the crazy idea to quit her job as a dental assistant and become a longarm quilter. Without really knowing what a longarm machine was, she spent a day at a longarm dealer's shop and walked out after purchasing a Gammill machine. Natalia's passion for quilting and being creative has grown each day since.

Whether it's working on an intense show quilt or a simple baby quilt, Natalia has become a real quilting addict. She has won numerous awards for her work and has been featured on Moda Bake Shop and in *Quiltmaker, Fons & Porter's Love of Quilting, American Patchwork & Quilting,* and McCall's *Quick Quilts magazines.* Natalia is author of *Beginner's Guide to Free-Motion Quilting,* co-author of *Modern One-Block Quilts,* and a contributor to *Fresh Fabric Treats, Modern Blocks,* and *Sweet Celebrations with the Moda Bake Shop Chefs.*

Photo by Whitnee North

Kathleen Jasperson Whiting has been sewing as long as she can remember; her mother and grand-mother always had a quilting project going on, so naturally sewing became part of her life. Kathleen is from Boise, Idaho. She has lived the past 35 years in a small town in the Utah mountains, where she raised 5 children and now is grandma to 7 grand-daughters and a grandson. Sewing, quilting, designing, and decorating are her passions.

In 2009, Kathleen was named the first *McCall's* Quilt Design Star. She has won numerous awards for her quilts, and her designs have been published in *McCall's Quilting, Quiltmaker, American Patchwork & Quilting,* and *McCall's Quick Quilts magazines.* Kathleen is co-author of *Modern One-Block Quilts.*

Also by the authors:

stashBOOKS®

fabric arts for a handmade lifestyle

If you're craving beautiful authenticity in a time of mass-production...Stash Books is for you. Stash Books is a line of how-to books celebrating fabric arts for a handmade lifestyle. Backed by C&T Publishing's solid reputation for quality, Stash Books will inspire you with contemporary designs, clear and simple instructions, and engaging photography.

ctpub.com